FAITH
in the Family
A Handbook for Parents

By Dr Anne Burke-Gaffney Bsc. MA, PhD
& Fr Marcus Holden MA (Oxon), STL

CATHOLIC TRUTH SOCIETY

Publishers to the Holy See

website: www.CTSbooks.org

Published 2013 by The Incorporated Catholic Truth Society, 40-46 Harleyford Road London SE11 5AY
Tel: 020 7640 0042 Fax: 020 7640 0046. © 2013 The Incorporated Catholic Truth Society.

ISBN 978 1 86082 860 7

Inside Illustrations from Holy Ghost Catholic Primary School

Contents

Introduction 5

Creation and Created

1. God and Creation 9

2. Angels 14

3. Saints 17

4. Holy Souls 21

5. Mary 25

Knowing God

6. Prayer 31

7. The Mass 37

8. Confession 46

9. The Bible 51

10. Catholic Devotions 55

Catholic Life and Times

11. Advent and Christmas 63

12. Lent and Easter 69

13. Children's Literature 77

14. Cultivating Virtue 80

15. Evangelisation and Vocation 85

by Cecilia Bogle, Year 5

Introduction

A young girl was walking along a narrow, winding country road with her family. She stopped in front of a 'dangerous bends' road sign and announced, to whoever might be listening: "Life is like that; like a journey on a winding road. "She walked a bit further and then stopped again; this time at a 'road narrows' sign. "Sometimes it's like that too," the girl went on. "The road gets really narrow and the journey gets very difficult. But that's okay because at the end it's really exciting because you get to go to heaven, and you can see God and Jesus and all the saints!" she enthused. This true story is interesting on two accounts. First, the young girl is right, life is a journey towards God; a journey which parents help children make by encouraging them to build an honest and lasting relationship with God. Second, the story illustrates the innate spirituality of children, a concept that often perplexes parents and can sometimes make them feel ill-equipped to nurture such a wonderful gift.

There are several ways parents can help children to grow in faith: by living and loving the faith because children often come to love what we love; by praying for and with our children; by making our home a place of faith and strong Christian values. A supportive environment beyond the home in schools and parishes is also enormously valuable. Finally, parents help children grow in faith through a willingness to have a go at answering their questions. It's not about always, instantly supplying the correct answers, but about having the courage to try, as a part of normal, everyday conversation.

Faith in the Family is a handbook for parents that summarises key aspects of the faith in a question and answer format. The questions were asked by children aged between seven and eleven, but resemble those asked by children of all ages. The answers provide a few opening words with which you might reply to a child's question; and then further information that explores the topic in more detail. We very much hope that this approach will give parents the confidence to try answering the (often challenging) faith-related questions that children ask.

The aim of this handbook is thus three-fold. To help parents:

1. Understand better some of the key aspects of Catholic faith and life.

2. Answer children's faith-related questions.

3. Provide some thoughts to reflect on and practical suggestions to help cement faith in the family.

We wish to thank all the parents and children of Holy Ghost Church and School, Balham, London, who helped in many ways to bring this publication to life; especially the parents who attended our parish-based Faith in the Family course, and the children of the school for their artwork. Finally, we wish to thank our own parents who handed on the faith to us and the next generation who asked the questions!

31st January 2013, Feast of St John Bosco

CREATION AND CREATED

by Joseph Brown, Year 4

1. God and Creation

Who made God?

Nobody made God. God has always existed. God is infinite which means 'has no beginning or end'. God has always existed even before the beginning of the universe; and will always exist, no matter what happens to the universe. We cannot see God because God is pure spirit. Mysterious though it might seem, God is also three persons together. The first person is God the Father, who created heaven and earth and everything in it. The second person is God the Son, Jesus, who came so that God could be near us on earth, show us how much he loved us and, ultimately, who died so that one day we could be with him in heaven. The third person is God the Holy Spirit who comes to us first in baptism and stays with us always; helping us, keeping us safe and leading us to heaven.

How did God make the world?

We believe that God made the world out of nothing. The Latin phrase for this is 'ex nihilo'. The vast majority of scientists now also think that the universe began at a single moment, commonly called the Big Bang. The opening words of Genesis: "In the beginning, God created the heavens and the earth" fit well with the Big Bang Theory. The word 'day' in the book of Genesis is probably not a literal 24-hour day. Here 'day' more likely means a period of time and stands for the time taken to create the world. It is put in a way that we can more easily understand. Genesis tells us the order in which the world was created; it is not an exact timescale. In fact, calculations suggest that the Big Bang and the beginning of the universe happened about fourteen billion years ago. Earth came into existence about four billion years ago and the first fossil records of possible ancestors of modern man date from about 195,000 years ago. Even before all these things God was neither young nor old; he was always there and everything came from him, and without him nothing could have come or remain here now.

Why did God make us?

After God created the world and all its creatures, God wanted to create something incredibly special 'in his own image and likeness' (us) so that he could share creation. God created human beings with a material body and a non-material (or spiritual) soul which is the part of us most like God. God hoped that each person would come to know and love him; and also serve him, because when you love someone you look for ways to help and serve them. However, God gave us free will so we could choose, without being forced, how we would respond. God hopes that each of us will choose to love him because no matter how many of us have been born and will be born, the love we each give to God is completely and utterly unique. Following our own special journeys through life, God hopes that each of us will come to centre our lives on him and in the end, be truly united with him in heaven.

Were Adam and Eve real?

Whilst the names Adam (from the Hebrew word meaning 'man') and Eve (meaning 'life') are symbolic, what is real is that at some point in creation God stepped in and made something fundamentally new when he gave a spiritual soul to a material being and created the first human beings. The soul made human beings fundamentally different from the plants and other animals because they could understand and speak and they were free. God created a home for them on earth in a beautiful place that we know as the Garden of Eden. In the beginning, Adam and Eve had a very close friendship with God and loved him very much. They had many special gifts of knowledge and were to be preserved from ever dying. God hoped that they would choose to go on loving him, and to look after creation and teach their children to do the same.

Why did God create Satan?

Satan, originally called Lucifer, was one of God's angels, who like all the angels was created with free will to choose to serve God, or not; tragically, Lucifer chose not to. Satan was proud and wanted to be greater than God. Some of the other angels chose to side with Satan against God. There was a big battle in heaven in which Archangel Michael led the good angels in a fight against the bad (fallen) angels. This was the first ever struggle of good against evil. The good angels won and the bad angels were banished from heaven to hell, a place of permanent separation from God.

Why did Adam and Eve spoil everything?

God gives all human beings free will to choose how to respond to his love, and Adam and Eve chose to disobey God and spoilt their friendship with him. Before judging Adam and Eve it is worth wondering whether we might also have chosen to act as they did. It is unlikely that Adam and Eve would have known the far-reaching consequences of their actions beforehand and it is a real lesson for all of us in learning to trust God; even if we do not immediately fully understand the reasons behind what is being asked of us.

The sequence of events described figuratively in Genesis is one of the best known Bible stories. Satan, who like any angel can appear in a material form if necessary, appeared in the Garden of Eden as a serpent and succeeded in persuading Eve and through her, Adam, to disobey God. They chose to eat the fruit "of the tree of knowledge of good and evil" (Gn 2:17), which was the one thing that God had asked them not to do. The consequences were truly dreadful. Adam and Eve knew straightaway that they had damaged their friendship with God and each other. But even worse, because of the seriousness of their disobedience, their action brought suffering, evil, death and destruction into the world for everyone who comes after them. Despite the enormous gulf that came between God and his people, God never stopped loving them and promised them a saviour in the future (who we now know is Jesus) to help bring the people back to him.

What is my soul?

The soul is our spiritual nature and is the part of us which most resembles God. God created us body and soul and while the human body most likely developed in stages like everything else, the human soul is always created directly by God. Every human being receives a soul at the very first moment of their existence and has dignity and rights as a human being from the very beginning, including the right to life. The soul is united to the body and is the part of us that allows us to understand and to choose freely. As our soul is spiritual and not material it cannot be passed on from generation to generation. When we die our soul separates from our body and goes to heaven (sometimes through purgatory) or hell where it waits for the final reunion with the body that will happen at the end of time. What we do and how we choose, with our free will, to act in this life affects where we shall be forever.

Why did God make bad people?

God neither made bad people nor created evil. God made all beings (humans and angels) good and with free will to choose how to act. Unfortunately, some beings that were created good chose to act against God (Satan, the fallen angels and Adam and Eve) and their wrong deeds damaged the goodness of the created world. After Adam and Eve disobeyed God (we call this 'the fall') the tendency to act in the wrong way became a part of human nature. As a result evil and wrong doing continue throughout the history of mankind.

Why does God allow earthquakes, floods and hurricanes to happen?

It is always very hard to understand why it seems that God allows natural disasters to happen, particularly those in which many people die. It might be that some of the powerful forces within the universe could be part of an ongoing creative process, given the explosive way science tells us that the world was created. The way we tamper with our environment, whilst not causing them, might also contribute to some natural phenomena and disasters. Sometimes there might also be a link between sin and the disruption we see in nature. However, that does not mean that we should assume that all disasters are a punishment for the people involved. God allows the world and forces of nature to develop in their own way. Occasionally, the number of people who die in a natural disaster is linked to human mistakes and error, such as when houses are built without proper earthquake protection.

Why is it important to look after the world?

We have a responsibility to care for God's creation, both the environment and all living creatures. That we are all part of creation links us together and should remind us to think often about how we treat or mistreat the rest of the created world. All creation is good; God loves creation and so should we. Sadly, our relationship with the earth has become one in which we want to be in charge, and we sometimes act as if the world and creation is ours to do with as we wish. When God put human beings high up in the order of creation he very much hoped that they would love and respect the rest of creation, not mistreat and damage it as we so often do.

We frequently need to remind ourselves that we are a part of the whole of creation. We need to remember that material creation comes from God just as much as spiritual creation. Without the stories in the book of Genesis we might easily forget that the world is connected to God. We might also forget that the universe came from somewhere and is going somewhere. We might sadly start to think of the world as mainly bad or evil, forgetting that the cosmos comes from love and was all good before evil crept in. We need to do our best to look after creation and fight against evil.

Points to ponder

- How do we talk to our children about God?

- How would we explain the story of creation to our children?

- How do our children understand themselves and their place in the world?

Practical application

- Take a few moments to talk to your children about:

  ○ How God wants to be their closest friend and whatever happens this will always be so.

  ○ How we need to look after and care for the world we live in and respect the rest of creation.

- Pray as a family about environmental issues; maybe a topic that is in the news, an event local to you; or something bigger, like global warming or deforestation. If you feel strongly about an environmental issue, pray about it. The power of prayer to change events should never be underestimated.

- With your children, think about the products you buy. How were they produced? Seemingly small gestures to buy only those products from the developing world where decent working conditions are supported and prices are fair, can make a difference.

2. Angels

What are angels?

An angel is a pure immortal spirit and as a rule, we cannot see them. However, angels can take bodily form if it is necessary for us to see them. God created angels before humans and gave them all their knowledge at once. So unlike us, angels do not have to learn anything! The English word 'angel' comes from a Greek word *'angelos'* meaning 'messenger'. This reminds us that angels carry out missions on earth. Angels are usually shown with wings, suggesting that they can deliver God's message swiftly. Another job of the angels is to adore God and they are often shown with haloes to show holiness, indicating that they are in heaven with God. An understanding and awareness of angels can help us to appreciate the spiritual realm that surrounds us, and can act as a guard against the lie that we have no souls. The angels protect us from evil.

Do angels really exist?

Yes, angels are not a myth; their existence is a dogma of the Catholic faith (revealed by God and declared by the Church to be true). For some people experience confirms their belief in angels and for others it simply seems likely that God would have made spiritual beings. Much of what we know about angels is based on Scripture. Angels are mentioned hundreds of times in the Bible. In the Old Testament there are angels who guard the entrance to the Garden of Eden after Adam and Eve are expelled. There are the angels that Jacob sees in a dream going up and down a ladder reaching to heaven. In the New Testament, the Archangel Gabriel announces to Mary that she will bear a son, Jesus. Angels appear to the shepherds on the hillside and tell them of Jesus' birth. Other angels in the Nativity story instruct the Wise Men not to go back to Herod. An angel appears to Joseph in a dream and tells him to flee to Egypt with Jesus and Mary, to escape Herod's massacre of little children. Angels also appear at the temptation of the Lord in the desert, his sufferings in Gethsemane, and the Resurrection and Ascension.

How many angels are there?

It is impossible to know how many angels there might be, but St Thomas Aquinas described nine different types, based on Scripture and tradition referred to as: seraphims, cherubims, thrones, dominations, virtues, powers, principalities, archangels and angels. The seraphims and cherubims are the closest to God. The seraphims sing God's praises in heaven and the cherubims guard heaven. Guardian angels and archangels have missions to earth.

There are three archangels mentioned in the Bible: Michael, Gabriel and Raphael. The '- el' at the end of their name is a name for God in Hebrew and indicates their connection with the divine. Michael means 'who is like God' and is the archangel that defends the faith because he is the one who throws the fallen angels out of heaven. Gabriel means 'power of God' and is God's main messenger. Raphael means 'medicine of God' and brings God's healing; in the Old Testament, he cures Tobit of blindness. They are called archangels because of the importance of their missions.

Why do we have guardian angels?

Every one of us has a guardian angel from the very first moment of our existence that stays with us the whole of our life to help, guide, guard and protect us. Angels have power in our world, but will only do what God wants them to do. Guardian angels are spoken of in the Old Testament, in the Psalms: "For you has he commanded his angels, to keep you in all your ways" (Ps 90:11). Also in the New Testament, in Matthew's Gospel (18:10), Jesus tells us that we have angels who look after us who also see God: "See that you never despise any of these little ones, for I tell you that their angels in heaven are continually in the presence of my Father in heaven."

Can we talk to our guardian angels?

Yes, we can talk to our guardian angels by speaking to them in our mind, or occasionally out loud! Our angels can always hear us, but that does not mean that they will take orders. Many saints like St Josemaria Escriva and holy people such as Blessed Pope John XXIII have enjoyed great friendship with their guardian angels whose help they sought frequently. Generally, our guardian angels do not speak to us directly, but instead help us to know what we need to do, for example by bringing an image to our mind or jogging our memories.

Why do we say the guardian angel prayer?

We say the guardian angel prayer, "Angel of God, my guardian dear, to whom God's love commits me here, ever this day/night be at my side, to light, to guard, to rule and guide. Amen" to ask our angel to be with us; to help us see clearly what we need to do each day (to light), to protect us from danger (to guard), to help us know the right thing to do (to rule) and to lead us through each day (to guide). We can say the guardian angel prayer morning and night.

Our angels look after us so well that often we do not even know the danger we might have faced without their protection. We should always thank our angels for their protection at the end of each day. In our prayers, we should also ask our guardian angels for advice in solving problems. Many of the saints never did anything without first asking advice of their guardian angels. Also, when we are tempted to do something wrong we can ask our guardian angels to help us not to. Our guardian angels see all that we do! We can also ask our guardian angels to join their prayers with ours and bring them to God.

Points to ponder

- How often do we remember to ask our guardian angel for help?

- Do we have memories of angels acting in our lives and giving us protection?

- Do our children understand the importance of angels?

Practical application

- The feast days of the angels, 29th September for the three archangels, and 2nd October, the feast of the guardian angels, could be celebrated in the family with a special treat.

- Say the guardian angel prayer with your children; if possible, in the morning and evening.

- Perhaps have a picture or statue of an angel in your home as a reminder to every family member to ask their guardian angels for help and protection.

- Sometimes make a habit of asking your guardian angel aloud for help to encourage the practice in your children; perhaps just for something simple like finding a parking space!

- If you are reading Bible stories with your children, make a note of those featuring angels. How many can you find?

3. Saints

How many saints are there?

There are countless numbers of saints, heaven is full of them. A saint is any person who has died and is now in heaven with God. A canonised saint is a person who the Church officially acknowledges to be in heaven. In addition to all the canonised saints there are many other saints including most probably members of our own family and friends. On 1st November, 'All Saints Day' is celebrated to remember all the saints, known and unknown, in heaven. The term 'communion of saints' is used to refer, collectively, to the faithful on earth trying to become saints, the souls in purgatory who hope to go to heaven soon and the saints already in heaven.

To be a saint it is not necessary to be famous or perform spectacular deeds. Anyone who follows Jesus, faithfully, can be a saint. That is why we are told that we are all called to be saints (that is, to be holy). This is called 'the universal call to holiness'. It does not mean that we have to say an extraordinary number of prayers, just that we try to do our very best in everything we do each day and rely totally on God's help. When Blessed Mother Teresa of Calcutta was asked what is was like being called a saint, she said: "There is nothing extraordinary about being holy. It is simply a duty for you and for me. The universal call to holiness consists of a commitment to the faith, loving and serving God and others and helping with the saving work of Christ."

Who were the first saints?

After the Blessed Virgin Mary and the original disciples of the Lord, the first saints recognised by the early Church were martyrs; people who were killed because of their faith. By AD 100 Christians had begun to honour other Christians who had died. These early saints were usually chosen by public acclaim rather than by any formal process.

How are saints made?

Since the 10th century, the Church has used a formal process called 'canonisation' to determine who is a saint. Canonisation does not make saints - God makes them - but the Church uses this long and complicated process to make sure that these people really are in heaven with God. When the title of saint is conferred on someone it declares that a person lived a holy life, is in heaven and can be honoured as a saint. Canonisation is certain and unchangeable, which is why it is such a long and complicated process. In order to give a clear perspective on the candidate, the process of canonisation does not usually start until many years after the death of a Catholic whom people regard as holy. When the canonisation process finally begins, there are four steps:

The first step is that the local bishop of the area where the candidate died investigates his or her life and writings for evidence that they lived a holy life to a 'heroic degree' (or suffered martyrdom) and also for their faithfulness to true doctrine. At the end of this stage the person is referred to as a 'servant of God' and all the documentation is passed to Rome.

In the second step, the Church chooses a panel of scholars to study the candidate. When the panel, together with the cardinals of the Congregation for the Causes of Saints, approve the cause the Pope proclaims the candidate 'venerable'. This is the title for a person considered to be holy by the Church, but who is not yet a saint. A 'venerable' does not yet have a feast day and the Church has made no pronouncements on the certainty of the person's presence in heaven. However, prayer cards can be printed to encourage people to pray for a miracle through the intercession of the candidate.

The third step is beatification and requires evidence of one miracle (except for martyrs who have been killed because of their faith), obtained as a result of specific petition to the candidate. Miracles are considered proof that the candidate is in heaven and can intercede, on our behalf, before God. When the Pope proclaims the candidate beatified or 'blessed', the person can be venerated or honoured in the countries or places specifically associated with him or her.

Finally, one more miracle is required for the Pope to canonise the saint and then the saint's feast day can be celebrated throughout the world.

Why do we have saints?

The saints set us good examples that can help us live good lives. Also, the saints can pray for us before God if we ask them to. When we pray to a saint we are simply asking them to join their prayers with ours. We ask the saints to help us in the same way that we might ask a friend to help us with a task. Certain saints are invoked for particular causes with which they are linked. Traditionally, St Anthony is the saint we turn to when we have lost something. St Rita is an extraordinarily powerful intercessor for difficult or seemingly impossible cases. St Rita is also a patron saint of families! Different saints acting as patrons for different causes can be viewed as God's way of 'delegating' jobs within the family of the Church. However, it is important to recognise that saints do not work outside God's providence (that is, God's oversight and what God desires for each of us). Whilst the Church teaches that it is not necessary to have a devotion to any particular saint, many families and children do.

Why do saints have feast days?

Saints have feast days (most often the day they died and joined God in heaven) because it gives us a special day to remember and honour them. St Bernard of Clairvaux tells us that whilst the saints do not need our veneration, honouring them is our way of "loving those who love us". We can honour saints not only by celebrating their feast days, but by calling on them in prayer and naming our children after them. An early Christian custom, still popular in some Catholic countries today, is to celebrate name days, the feast of the saint after whom you are named. If a child learns to pray regularly to their patron saint then the feast day will be even more exciting. Getting to know the saints, praying to them and celebrating their feast days are all customs that can help children to understand how great and important it is to become holy.

Points to ponder

- What do we understand by 'the universal call to holiness'? Do we recognise that it can be achieved by striving to love God and others through our commitment to our ordinary daily tasks and chores?

- Do our children understand that God wants them to be saints? How might we help them?

Practical application

- As a family, make a list of the saints that are most important to you. Find ways of marking those days; an extra small treat might be one way.

- Include your family list of saints in your children's night time prayers.

- As a family visit a place associated with a saint; maybe one of the saints in your family list of saints, or a saint local to your area.

- Encourage your children to explore the stories of their favorite saints. There are many good children's books about saints that can them help them to get to know, love and pray to their patron, or favourite saints. Some helpful books on saints are:

  ○ *The Lion Treasury of Saints: From the Time of Jesus to the Present Day* (David Self) lists the saints in historical order.

  ○ *Loyola Kids Book of Saints* (Amy Welborn) divides the lives of saints into themes based on the main quality of the saint that make them models of Christian living.

  ○ *Saints for Young Readers for Every Day: Vol. 1 and 2* (Susan Helen Wallace and Melissa Wright) gives the life of a saint, together with a brief reflection, for each day of the year.

  ○ *101 Saints and Special People* (Vera Schauber and Michael Schindler) also looks at saints through the year.

  ○ *Making Friends with the Saints* (Thérèse Boucher), is another excellent book in which the author suggests, using examples from her own experience, numerous ways of getting to know and love the saints.

  ○ There are also many good DVDs on the lives of saints.

4. Holy Souls

What happens when we die?

When we die our body and soul separates, and as our soul cannot stay on earth without a body it goes one of three ways: to heaven, hell or purgatory. Heaven and hell are final destinations and once there, that is where we stay. Purgatory is where souls that are not quite yet perfect enough to be with God in heaven go. All souls that go to purgatory (we call them the holy souls) are guaranteed to go to heaven in the end. At the moment of our death, Jesus judges how we lived our lives on earth; not just whether we kept the commandments and avoided sin, but what good things we did. The most important factor is whether we are friends with God; we call this being in a 'state of grace'.

Is hell real?

Hell is real but it is not a fiery location at the centre of the earth as some have thought. Hell is a state of being; a state of suffering and pain for all eternity, a state of total absence of love. We do not know with certainly who goes to hell, but we do know that God does not want anyone to go there. Sadly, sometimes people choose out of free will not to be with God. God never forces anyone to be with him in this life or the next.

What is heaven like?

Heaven is being in the presence of God at all times. When we see God we experience eternal happiness and unending joy. Heaven is for those souls who during their life have been transformed into the likeness of Jesus; and for those who have been made perfect following their passage through purgatory. Heaven is our homeland; it is where we are meant to be and where God wants us to choose to be.

What is purgatory?

Purgatory, unlike heaven and hell, is not a final destination after death, but it is where many souls pass through on their journey to heaven. Purgatory helps to transform us if, when we die, we are not quite ready for heaven. Purgatory exists because many of us spend our time on earth doing what we want to do rather than what God would like us to do. When we die, we might be at peace with God and have gone to confession regularly, but we also need to make up for the damage our sins have caused. We might manage to do this on earth but, if not, we have the chance to make amends for our sins in purgatory instead. The function of purgatory is to change the state of the soul so that it is perfect to be with God in heaven. Someone once said that purgatory was a bit like a dry cleaner for souls! Instead of removing stains from clothes, purgatory removes stains from your soul. One small child said that purgatory was the hard way to heaven; a bit like climbing the mountain to get to the top rather than taking a cable car!

Why do we pray for the holy souls?

We pray for the holy souls in purgatory because our prayers help them to get to heaven. A soul in purgatory stays there until it is perfect and ready for heaven, but they cannot do anything further to help themselves. However, we can: we can pray for them often. The greatest prayer of all is the Mass and it is good to have Masses offered for our deceased friends and relatives at any time, but particularly on the anniversary of their death. The month of November is dedicated to the holy souls and this is a special time for remembering them. Also, 2nd November is All Souls Day and is the day that we especially remember our friends and relatives who have died.

Can we avoid purgatory?

Yes, there are several ways we can avoid or reduce our time in purgatory. First, by reducing the number of sins we commit (avoiding mortal ones and reducing the amount of venial sins); and secondly, by making up for the things we have done wrong. One way to do this is to do penance which, as St Thérèse of Lisieux pointed out, can be as simple as doing small tasks very well, giving up certain things or bearing suffering patiently. Going to confession, communion and Mass regularly is also very beneficial, and so is receiving the blessing of the sick if you are seriously ill. Finally, we can pray often that we will go straight to heaven. It is certain that if our love for God is not perfect when we die we will to need to go to purgatory. No one knows when they will die so it is really important to try hard each day with all our tasks and to grow in holiness.

What will happen when the world ends?

We have no idea when the world will end or how it will happen. The early Christians sometimes thought that it would end in their lifetime but it did not and more than two thousand years later we are still here. These early Christians remind us that we should look forward to Jesus coming again at the end of time. As his friends, we should not be afraid because he will solve all our problems, and take away all the evil and suffering in the world. We do know that when it does happen, souls and bodies will be reunited and that there will be a final judgement at which we will all be present. The verdict we receive when we die cannot change, but this is the time when everyone will know what happened to everyone else.

Points to ponder

• How do our children understand death? Understandably, we are extremely sad when someone close to us dies, but can we take some comfort from knowing that their soul lives on forever and that they will rise again like Jesus?

• How would we talk to our children about heaven, hell and purgatory?

Practical application

• Try to pray for the holy souls often. Perhaps include the prayer for the holy souls in your daily prayers: Eternal rest grant unto them, O Lord, and let perpetual light shine upon them. May the souls of the faithful departed, through the mercy of God, rest in peace. Amen.

• Remember deceased family members on their anniversary by requesting a Mass to be said for them.

• Include all your deceased friends and relatives in the altar list of the dead in your parish church during November.

• Make little sacrifices for the holy souls during the month of November. Perhaps encourage your children to eat a meal or food they do not particularly like without complaining.

• If it is possible, visit the grave of a friend or relative on their anniversary or during the month of November. If not, perhaps light a candle or say a decade of the Rosary for them.

• If you hear of a tragic accident, pray for the souls of those who have died.

• Pray often to go straight to heaven when you die.

by Faith Blackden, Year 6

5. Mary

Who were Mary's parents?

We do not know very much about Mary's family, but traditions say that her mother and father were called Anne and Joachim. Often statues of St Anne show her as an old lady. We think that Anne and Joachim were quite old when Mary was born. In fact, Mary's birth was a miracle because Anne and Joachim did not think that they would ever have a baby. Often pictures of St Anne show her pointing to a book, teaching Mary all about the faith. It is good to ponder the fact that Jesus had a grandfather and a grandmother and then perhaps to pray for our own grandparents and ancestors.

What does "full of grace" mean in the Hail Mary?

"Full of grace" in the Hail Mary refers to the fact that Mary was born without original sin. Everyone else has original sin at birth because it became part of human life after Adam and Eve disobeyed God. God loved Mary so much and wanted her to be the mother of his Son so he gave her the maximum amount of grace (that is, God living within) from the very beginning of her life. This is why we pray "Hail Mary, full of grace". Not only did God love Mary, but Mary also loved God with her whole heart, mind and soul, as we are asked to do in the first commandment. Mary is a really excellent role model; she shows us how we can try to be perfect, to be like Jesus.

How did Mary die?

We believe that Mary did not die, instead her body and soul went up into heaven. It is logical that Mary did not die because death is the result of original sin and as Mary was not born with original sin she would not die as everyone else does. We refer to Mary's passage to heaven as the Assumption, not to be confused with Jesus' Ascension into heaven.

Why do we pray to Mary?

When we say we pray to Mary, what we mean is that we ask her to join her prayers with ours. We give her praise and we ask her to look after us. We ask her to help us as we would ask a good friend. Mary helps us make our prayers clearer, as when a small child cannot quite form his or her words and the mother is the one person who understands what they are trying to say. In a similar way, Mary understands our needs, and presents them clearly and simply to Jesus. The best example of this is the Wedding Feast of Cana. In the middle of the wedding the wine runs out and the servants are worrying about what to do. When Mary sees the confusion she turns to Jesus and says simply, "They have no wine." Through our prayers, Mary also helps to bring us closer to Jesus. This is seen physically in the Bible when, with Jesus in her womb, Mary visits her cousin Elizabeth. Mary also draws the shepherds and the Wise Men to Jesus. Is it necessary to always ask Mary to help us and to join her prayers with ours? No; but as God has given us Mary as an intercessor and our spiritual mother, why would we not want to ask her to help us?

Why do some people 'see' Mary?

Over the centuries, Mary has appeared to an individual or small group of people in different places all over the world to encourage us to stay faithful to Jesus. We call such sightings of Mary 'apparitions' and they occur when an image imprints on the senses. Usually, when it happens, Mary asks us to pray to Jesus and do penance. Often apparitions occur at difficult times in history. For example, Mary appeared to three little children in Fatima, Portugal, during the terrible times of the First World War. Sometimes an apparition leads to a new devotion. When Mary appeared to St Catherine Labouré, a Sister of Charity who lived in Paris in the 19th century, she asked her to have a new medal made called the Miraculous Medal with the words, "Oh Mary, conceived without sin" inscribed on it.

Why do we say the Rosary?

We say the Rosary because the word means 'garland of roses' and so praying the Rosary is a metaphorical way of giving flowers or a gift to Mary. The Rosary is the most popular and well-loved of devotions to Mary. History suggests that the Rosary, in its present form, originated from St Dominic. Our Lady appeared to him and taught him to pray the Rosary. However, it is likely that the idea of a Rosary dates from before this. Originally, monks prayed all 150 Psalms. If you could not read, you prayed the Rosary instead, which had an equivalent number of prayers: 15 mysteries with 10 Hail Marys each makes 150 Hail Marys. The original 15 mysteries were 5 joyful, sorrowful and glorious mysteries. Blessed Pope John Paul II added the luminous mysteries to cover Christ's public life. The sequence of prayers is recited whilst, at the same time, meditating on the life of Mary and Jesus. It is usual to say one set of mysteries (that is, five decades) at a time. The Rosary is not supposed to be a mindless repeating of a series of prayers. It is a special, thoughtful technique that joins together the mind, the voice, and the senses of touch and sight.

Points to ponder

• How important is Mary in our lives? Could we ask Mary, mother of the Holy Family, to look after our family?

• Could we make Mary a role model for us and our children?

• Do we pray the Rosary as a family? If not, could we start by praying a decade of the Rosary, perhaps once a week, with other family members?

Practical application

• In stages, teach your children to pray the Rosary. If you feel you need to find a way into start praying the Rosary and suggesting it to your family, October is the month of the Holy Rosary and a great time to begin. There are two parts to praying the Rosary: knowing and saying the prayers and reflecting or meditating on the mysteries. Maybe start by familiarising your children with each of the mysteries, without saying the prayers. Next, take one mystery, reflect on it for a few minutes and then say one decade of the Rosary. Sometimes this might be all you manage, another time you might say two decades or perhaps you will have time for all five mysteries of the day (Joyful on Mondays and Saturdays; Sorrowful on Tuesdays and Fridays; Luminous on Thursdays, and Glorious on Wednesdays and Sundays).

- There are lots of other beautiful prayers to Mary including the Hail, Holy Queen and the *Memorare*. Perhaps try to teach your children some of these other Marian prayers. Choose a day - maybe Saturday, the day dedicated to Our Lady - to say these extra prayers.

- Encourage your children to think of Mary as an extra mother to whom they can turn when they need help.

- Apart from prayers there are lots of different practical ways of honouring Mary. If you have a statue of Our Lady you might like to place a small flower or a candle by it on her feast days, such as her birthday on 8th September and the Feast of the Immaculate Conception on 8th December.

- The month of May is traditionally devoted to Mary and one way to mark this is to make a special garden of flowers for Mary. It does not have to be a real one! One idea is to take a piece of card and to suggest that family members draw a flower on it when they have done a good deed, or helped a family member or friend in some small way. By the end of May, Mary will have a beautiful garden!

KNOWING GOD

by Emmy Raines, Year 4

6. Prayer

Why do we pray?

One reason we pray is because it is the way we have a conversation with God. When we talk to a friend we tell them about ourselves and what we are doing, and we listen to what they have to say and find out about them. The more we get to know a person, the better friends we can become and the more we grow to love them. The same is true with God. The more we pray, the more we get to know God. The more we get to know God, the better friends we become and the more we love him. God knows us better than anyone else ever can, so he must love us more than anyone else. Because he loves us so much, we want to try to love him in return. This is another reason why we pray, because without prayer it is very difficult to love God. Prayer is the gift God gives us to help us get to know him better and to really come to love him.

A saint who lived in the 4th century called St Ephraem said that: "Birds fly, fish swim, people pray." This might seem strange; you would probably have expected him to say that "people walk" rather than "people pray." The point the saint is making is that praying is a vital part of being human. Praying is as much an essential part of our life as swimming is a basic feature of being a fish.

How do I pray?

There are several different ways we can pray and for convenience these can be called: vocal, mental and contemplative prayer.

Prayers such as the Our Father and Hail Mary are what we call vocal prayers and they play an important role in our prayer life. St Teresa of Avila, who lived in Spain in the 16th century, said that vocal prayers should be said with the greatest of devotion. That does not mean that we need to think about every single word every time we say the prayer, but we do need to make sure that our souls are turned towards God and that we are not just rattling off prayers without really thinking.

Another type of prayer is mental prayer, and is the way that we can talk to God about our everyday life and, in return, listen to what he has to say to us. This is probably the easiest form of prayer because we do not need to remember set words;

it simply comes from within ourselves. Mental prayer is not something complicated, difficult and reserved for the professionals. It is meant for everyone.

Here are some ideas to help you talk to God in mental prayer:

• Find a few minutes when you can be quiet and without distractions.

• Say "Hello" to God, as you would greet a friend.

• When you pray:

  ○ Tell God about your day; the things you have struggled with as well as the things that have gone well. Even though God knows everything he likes to hear it from you.

  ○ Pray about something specific: about your family or friends, a problem that needs to be solved, a decision that has to be made.

  ○ If you get distracted, maybe because a person comes to mind, pray for the person. If the distraction is something you need to remember to do, write it down and deal with it later.

  ○ Another approach to mental prayer is to take a gospel reading or the writings of a favourite saint. Think about how the words apply to you that day. For example, if it is the gospel story about the man whose friends lower him through the roof so he can be near to Jesus, you could pray: "How can I help bring my friends nearer to God?"

A third type of prayer is contemplative or silent prayer, silent, because we do not use words either aloud or in our minds to pray, we simply rest silently in God's presence. It might not be the easiest form of prayer for everyone, but perhaps start by taking a few moments every day just to try it. When we think about it, when we are with a very close friend we do not need to talk all the time, sometimes just being with them is sufficient. Having received a special grace some saints were able to pray in contemplation for hours.

Can I pray for anything?

Yes, as long as it is not for something wrong or that shows lack of respect for the Lord, like asking to do really well in a test for which we have done no work!

When we pray, it is helpful to remember that prayer has four parts. One way to remember these is using the mnemonic 'ACTS':

- A: Adoration is praising God simply because he is God. It is not about asking for things and striking deals with God. The angels in heaven praise God constantly and this is the best example of adoration.

- C: Contrition is being sorry for our sins. We should try to say sorry not because we are afraid of punishment, but because we are sad that we have hurt God with our sins.

- T: Thanksgiving is showing our appreciation for the blessings we have received from God.

- S: Supplication is asking God for help or favours for ourselves and others.

Can I pray anywhere?

Yes, but, if possible, it is a good idea to have a place and time (perhaps just a few minutes to start with) where we can be still and quiet enough to pray. We might ask, "Can I pray when I am lying down?" The answer is "Yes, of course", but that does not mean to say that you should lie down in order to pray!

Our goal should be to try to build prayer into our day and make it a necessity, like brushing our teeth. One way to do this is to start with times that we can say certain prayers: like a prayer in the morning, offering the day to God; grace at meal times and a prayer before we sleep. When we try to make a habit of these prayers, the time that we give to God will increase naturally. The benefits of giving certain times of the day to prayer also helps to make each day holy and forms the backbone or frame for our day on which everything else hangs.

Individual prayer is the bedrock of family prayer. A family is made up of a number of people, each called by God; each on his or her own unique journey towards truth and love. We cannot establish a relationship with God in our children or anyone else for that matter, but we can provide examples of praying with faith, humility and perseverance and we can teach prayers that will unfold in our children's understanding as they grow. The example of a parent who is sincerely seeking to pray will teach children more effectively than anything else. Teaching our children to pray is the single most important thing we can do for them. Finding time, however short, to pray as a family is also invaluable.

I can't hear God, so how do I know what he is saying?

God speaks to us though the good thoughts and inspirations that come to us during time spent in prayer, as well as other times during the day. Generally, we do not hear God as we would hear a human friend speaking to us. Instead, God responds to our prayers through the insights that come to us, perhaps prompted by a passage of Scripture we might have read.

As a rule of thumb, if our thoughts and inspirations are good and move us closer to God (for example, to be more patient with a family member or speak to a friend we have not spoken to for a while) then they are likely to be exactly what God desires us to do. Alternatively, if our thoughts or inspirations take us away from God, or do not fit with our life circumstances, then they are unlikely to be part of God's plan for us. If we are married with a family and living in England, God is not going to ask us to leave our family behind and go to be a missionary in Africa!

Does God always answer prayers?

Yes, but God never promised to answer our prayers exactly the way we want or in the time frame we often demand. Jesus just told us to be patient and ask without ceasing. Difficult though it can be for us to accept, God does know what is best for us and answers our prayers accordingly.

Points to ponder

- How do we understand prayer? How important is it in our lives? Could we make it more central to our lives?

- How do we talk to our children about prayer? Could we explain that prayer is the way that we talk to God, that God really wants to hear from us? Might we explain that we get to know and love God through prayer?

Practical application

• Spend some time, starting with just a few minutes, each day in mental prayer. Encourage other members of your family to do the same.

• Try to take a few moments to pray as a family, as your family circumstance allow; maybe start by saying grace at meal times or a morning offering together.

• Encourage your children to remember the four important parts of prayer when they pray. They can either use the mnemonic 'ACTS' or simply: "Please, thank you, I'm sorry and I love you!"

• Perhaps have little reminders around your home to encourage prayer. Maybe a small holy picture of Mary or a favourite saint in each room; it can even be placed discreetly above a door.

• Encourage your children to read, a few times a week, a short Bible story that they could reflect on when they take a few moments to pray at bedtime.

by Ellie Holliman, Year 5

7. The Mass

Why do we have to go to Mass?

There are very many reasons for going to Mass. Firstly, the Mass is the very best form of prayer; at Mass we have a special way to talk to God that we will not find anywhere else. When we are able to receive Holy Communion we receive God within us, and just after doing so is an especially good time to pray. Also, when we listen carefully to the readings, God will offer us help and direction and the Mass will give us strength to try to live our lives well. Another reason to go to Mass is that every time we do so we witness the sacrifice Jesus made when he died on the cross for us; so do we not owe it to God to go? Moreover, we go because Jesus asked us to at the Last Supper when he said "do this in memory of me." Finally, we go every Sunday (or Saturday evening) because the Church requires us to, unless illness or some other insurmountable difficulty prevents us.

Why do we bless ourselves with holy water when we go into the church?

One reason we bless ourselves with holy water on the way into the church is because it symbolises preparing (cleansing) ourselves before going to Mass; or even just going into the Church to say a prayer. It is a bit like washing our hands before eating a meal. Another reason we bless ourselves with holy water is to remind us of our baptism. Also, the physical act of making the sign of the cross reminds us that Jesus died on the cross for us. Saying silently, "In the name of the Father, and of the Son and of the Holy Spirit," helps us to remember the Trinity. Therefore, blessing ourselves with holy water is a simple but incredibly powerful gesture that, most of all, helps us to stop and pause for a moment before rushing into God's house, the Church.

Why do we genuflect?

We genuflect when we enter the church as a way of saying "hello" and acknowledging God's presence. We say hello when we visit a friend's house and it is equally important when we visit God's house. However, genuflecting is even more than just a mark of politeness. Genuflecting is an act of adoration, a way we show our love and devotion to God. We genuflect in the church when the tabernacle contains the Blessed Sacrament which is shown by a lit sanctuary lamp. On Good Friday or before the Easter Vigil we do not genuflect because the tabernacle is empty. Instead, we make a profound bow towards the altar because this is a sacred object that symbolises Christ. Also we do not genuflect before re-entering our place after communion because the body of Christ is now actually within us.

Why do we sit, stand and kneel at different times during the Mass?

Changing from one position to another helps us to keep our focus during Mass. If we were to sit the whole way through it might be very relaxing, but our minds are more likely to wander off and we could easily forget we are at Mass! We sit to hear the readings (except the Gospel) and the homily because sitting is a good position for listening. Standing and kneeling are both positions that can be used for prayer and show special respect and reverence (which is why we stand during the reading of the Gospel). There can be minor variations between countries as to when the congregation stands, sits and kneels.

Why do the altar servers carry a crucifix and candles at the start of Mass?

Altar servers lead the entrance procession carrying a crucifix because the crucifix is a sign of Jesus' presence and a reminder that the Mass is the sacrifice of Jesus. Also, the candles carried remind us that Jesus is the light of the world. For the same reason, candles are lit around the altar. The Mass begins with everyone standing up as the priest and servers enter.

Why does the priest kiss the altar?

First, the priest genuflects to the tabernacle, acknowledging that Jesus is really present there, and then he bows very low and kisses the altar as a sign of love and respect to Jesus, and to venerate relics of the saints placed in the altar. Next, the priest makes the sign of the cross because this is how we begin a prayer and the Mass is the greatest prayer of all.

Why do we all say "I confess"?

We say together the 'I Confess' prayer because it helps us to reflect on and say sorry for the wrong things we have done or said or even just thought; and also for all the things that we have forgotten to do. This prayer is near the beginning of the Mass because we need to say sorry to God and each other before we can move on.

Why do we ask God for mercy?

When we ask God for mercy we are asking him to forgive us. At Mass we say "Lord, have mercy; Christ, have mercy; Lord, have mercy", immediately after the 'I Confess' prayer because we are asking God to forgive us for the sins that we have just said we are sorry for. Our venial sins can be forgiven at this point to prepare us for the Mass and particularly Holy Communion. If we have committed mortal sins this prayer should prepare us for confession when we can be reconciled again with the Lord. Sometime we say the prayer in the original Greek of the Gospels which is a really powerful way to help us remember that we are connected with the early Christians. 'Kyrie' is the Greek word for 'Lord' and so we say, "Kyrie eleison, Christe eleison, Kyrie eleison"; we also call this prayer the 'Kyrie'.

Why do we not always say the Gloria?

The Gloria is a joyful prayer used on Sundays and feast days. We do not say the Gloria in Lent, which is a time of penance and sorrow; or Advent, a time of waiting for Jesus. At other times, we can say the Gloria after the 'I Confess' and the Kyrie because we have said sorry for our sins and asked for forgiveness and now, we move our focus away from us and back to God. The Gloria is the song the angels sang on Christmas night when Jesus was born. Angels are also with us now and we can imagine them around the altar praising God as we say the prayer during Mass.

What is the prayer the priest says before the readings?

Just before the readings the priest says a prayer called the 'Collect' or 'Opening Prayer'. The priest says this prayer to bring together all the prayers and intentions that we wish to pray for during the Mass. It is possible to see now that the first part of the Mass contains the four components of prayer: adoration, contrition, thanksgiving and supplication (remember 'ACTS'). The Gloria is a prayer of adoration and thanksgiving; the 'I Confess', of contrition and saying sorry; and the Collect, a prayer of supplication or asking God for help.

Why do we have so many Bible readings in Mass?

The readings of the Mass are the first part of what we call the 'Liturgy of the Word'. The readings span the whole history of God's people. On Sundays we listen to readings from four different parts of the Bible. The first reading is normally from the Old Testament (except during the Easter season) and is a story about God's people waiting for the coming of the Messiah. The first reading is chosen because it often links with the Gospel reading. The next reading is a Psalm, which also comes from the Old Testament and is a prayer of praise, thanksgiving or a plea for help. It is customary for the Psalms to be sung as they were in the ancient temple of Jerusalem. Jesus would have prayed the Psalms when he was growing up and also quoted from them a lot in his teaching. A second reading can come from the New Testament, either from the Acts of the Apostles or the letters that the apostles wrote to teach the people of the early Church about how to live and love like Jesus.

The final reading is from one of the four Gospels of the New Testament: Matthew, Mark, Luke or John. In solemn Masses the Gospel is often sung. The Gospel is Jesus speaking to us in his own words. We stand to hear the Gospel to help us remember that it is the most important of the readings and also as a mark of respect. The Gospel is introduced with the 'Alleluia' which is a Hebrew word that means 'Praise God'. As we prepare to listen to the Gospel it is customary to make the sign of the cross (with our thumb) on our forehead, lips and heart. This action represents asking God to help us understand what we hear (cross on our forehead); to talk to others about God (cross on our lips); and to love God and others (cross on our heart).

What does the priest speak about in his homily?

Generally, the priest speaks about the Gospel reading in his homily, to help us understand it and relate the story to our own lives. Even if we find it difficult to follow the entire homily, there will always be one or two points that we can understand. We can often use these ideas to guide and help us in the week ahead. After sitting down to listen to the homily, we stand up to say the Creed.

Why do we say the Creed?

We say the Creed because it contains the essential things that we, as Catholics, believe about God and what he has done for us. The word 'Creed' comes from the Latin word '*Credo*' which means, 'I believe'. When we say the Creed with others at Mass we say, "I believe" and not "we believe" because we are speaking our own mind; saying what I believe, not just copying the person next to us!

When we use the word 'believe' in the Creed we are not giving an opinion based on certain reasonable assumptions such as, "I believe I'll win the race" (based on the knowledge that I have trained the hardest and that generally, I'm the fastest!). In this race example, we are weighing up the evidence and giving an informed opinion based on it, but there is no absolute certainly in the statement. However, when we say "I believe" in the Creed, we are certain. We are saying "I believe" so completely that I would stake my life on the statements in the Creed being true.

Why do we have bidding prayers?

We have bidding prayers (or intercessions) so that we can pray for others during the Mass. Part of our efforts to love one another should be to pray for each other and the bidding prayers help us to do this in the context of the Mass, the greatest of all prayers. The bidding prayers are also called the prayers of the faithful. We pray for a whole range of intentions from the Pope, bishops and priests to the sick and suffering, for special needs in the world, for those who have died, for ourselves and our friends and families. The bidding prayers are the last part of the Liturgy of the Word; next, is the Liturgy of the Eucharist which is the very heart of the Mass.

Why are bread and wine carried to the altar?

The bread and wine can be carried to the altar in an offertory procession to represent the congregation bringing the gifts to the priest to offer them to God in our name. At other times they are brought directly by altar servers. As this is happening, we can also 'offer' to God, in our minds, everything that we have done during the week. This might include things that have gone well for us and also things with which we have struggled.

Why does the priest wash his hands?

The priest washes his hands with a few drops of water before preparing the gifts of bread and wine because it represents a custom from Jesus' time when the priests would wash their hands before sacrificing a lamb for Passover. It is reminiscent of when Pontius Pilate washed his hands before Jesus was crucified and therefore points to the Mass as a sacrifice. To prepare the gifts, the priest places the bread on a special plate called a paten and mixes the wine with a few drops of water. Mixing water with wine symbolises that Christ is both God (represented by the wine) and man (symbolised by water). Mixing water and wine also symbolises that we (the water) are to be brought close to Jesus (the wine).

In the liturgical sense, bread and wine symbolise food because they are the staple food of the human diet. As the food on our dinner table nourishes our body, so the food on the altar, which becomes the body and blood of Christ, nourishes our soul. Bread and wine also stand for everything we offer to God to be transformed.

Why do we say the 'Holy, holy, holy' prayer?

We say the 'Holy, holy, holy' prayer - also called the 'Sanctus' (which means 'holy' in Latin) - to remind us that a most holy miracle is about to happen before us when the bread and wine turn into the body and blood of Jesus. Also, the prayer reminds us that all the angels in heaven are praising Jesus with us at the altar (these are the 'hosts' of heaven referred to in the prayer). Furthermore, when we say "Hosanna in the highest", it unites us with the people of Jesus' time who joyously cheered and welcomed Jesus when he road into Jerusalem on Palm Sunday.

Why is a bell rung at the consecration?

A bell can be rung just before the priest speaks the words of the consecration (often at the moment when the priest stretches his hands over the gifts calling on the Holy Spirit to transform them), to remind us that are they are not just a symbol of Jesus; they actually become the body and blood of Christ. At the consecration the priest repeats the words and actions of Jesus at the Last Supper. He takes the bread and says: "This is my body; which will be given up for you." Then he holds the host up high showing it to all of us and offering it to God. This is a really good time to say a silent prayer to God for any special intentions you might have. The priest then takes the chalice of wine and speaks the words that Jesus spoke: "This is the chalice of my blood". The priest holds the chalice high offering it to God so that we can all see. The wine has become Jesus' precious blood. Again a bell can be rung to help us focus on this special moment. Jesus is really present and offers himself for us as he did two thousand years ago on the cross.

Why do we say the Our Father at Mass?

We say the Our Father shortly before communion because we are praying that we will come closer to God, who we are about to receive. Also, through the petitions of the Our Father, we pray that the obstacles that can sometimes prevent us from loving God and others will be removed. This is the prayer that Jesus himself taught us and is therefore a perfect prayer.

Why do we make the sign of peace?

On Sundays in the ordinary form of the Mass we make the sign of peace, usually by shaking hands, to share the peace we receive from Jesus with others. It also reminds us to be peacemakers in the world, and to work towards peace and unity with others.

Why does the priest break the host?

The priest breaks the host and puts a tiny piece of it into the chalice to represent the body and blood of Christ united in his living body. It also points back to an ancient tradition when a fragment of the host consecrated at the Papal Mass in Rome was taken to all the other churches in the city.

Why do we call Jesus the Lamb of God?

In the Mass we refer to Jesus as the 'Lamb of God' to acknowledge that Jesus sacrificed his life for our sins and makes that offering present for us at every Mass. The phrase 'Lamb of God' comes from the Jewish tradition of sacrificing a lamb at the Passover. John the Baptist addressed Jesus by saying, "Behold the Lamb of God who takes away the sin of the world."

How should we receive communion?

Generally, we have several choices about how we receive communion. We can stand or kneel, and we can receive the Blessed Sacrament in the palm of our hand or on our tongue. What is most important is that we receive Jesus well. We should walk respectfully up to the altar, focusing on who we are about to receive and not on who else is around us. If we wish to receive in our hands we make sure that they are clean. Also, we should place the host into our mouth before walking away from the altar; not only out of respect but because we do not want to drop Jesus on the floor.

Why do we pray after communion?

After we receive Holy Communion we have the living Jesus inside us. This is a fantastic time to pray because Jesus is incredibly close to us.

Where did the Mass get its name?

The Mass gets its name from the final words (when said in Latin) that the priest says which are: "*Ite missa est*" and means, 'Go, you are sent'. The Mass takes its name from this final phrase which points to its key purpose, namely, to equip us to go out into the world as Jesus' first disciples were sent, to spread the Gospel to others and to live out the life of Christ, whom we have received, in our everyday lives.

Points to ponder

• How do we prepare for Mass? Do we make sure that we plan when we will go to Mass and fit our other weekend arrangements around it?

• How do we prepare our children for Mass?

Practical application

- Perhaps try to look with your children at the readings for Mass before going; are they stories that they know? What do they think they mean?

- When time allows, take a moment or two to help your children begin to learn by heart some of the prayers of the Mass.

- Help your children understand the structure of the Mass.

- Persevere with taking children to Mass; do not be tempted to give up! The grace that your children receive from each Mass they attend is immeasurable.

- Plan in advance with your family when you will go to Mass. When your children see that going to Mass is important to you, it is more likely to become important to them.

- Expect older children in the family to go to Mass in order to set an example to the younger members.

- If possible, spend some time together as a family on Sunday. Make Sunday a special day with a special treat or meal.

8. Confession

Why do I need to go to confession?

Confession is like a bath for the soul; when our soul becomes grubby because of sin, confession cleans it. One person put it this way: when we are baptised, our soul gains a window to God and his light shines through this window bringing warmth and brightness to our life. When we sin, the window begins to get dirty or misty. As time goes on, we are not able to see God very well and his light can even be completely blocked by mortal sin. We need to find a way to clean the window; the way is called confession. When the window is cleaned and his light shines through it again, we can see God clearly once more.

In confession the priest stands in for Jesus; he acts as Christ. It is not the priest that absolves you from your sins but Jesus through the priest. Also, by our humble action of going to confession (and it is not easy to say our sins to another person, even if he does represent Jesus) we show that we are truly sorry for what we have done. When we go to confession we also receive grace (the restoration or development of the life of God within us) as part of the sacrament. The grace that we receive from going to confession is something very positive; it gives us extra strength to try not to sin again. Confession is the sacrament that reminds us that God loves us unconditionally and always forgives. Through going to confession we also learn to love and forgive others.

How do I know what sins I should say?

The best way to recall our sins and prepare for confession is to examine our conscience. God gives each of us a conscience to help us know the right way to act. Children's consciences need help to be properly formed; through our good example, by knowing the teaching of Christ and his Church, and through virtuous upbringing. Without this formation the conscience can be misguided by negative influences and dulled by compromises. When we examine our conscience we review how we have acted or behaved. When we reflect on how we live our life it is important to consider not only the things that we have done wrong, but also the ways we could have been more generous towards others, but chose not to be. The measure that we use when we reflect on our lives is the person and life of Christ.

A good way to examine our conscience, and to help our children to do the same, is to divide our life into a few distinct areas and take a look at each in turn to see how we are doing. The first area to consider is how we have acted towards God. Children can ask: "Do I pray every day; do I tell God I love him; do I thank God for all he has given me; did I pay attention in Mass; did I miss Mass on Sunday?"

The second area to think about is how we have acted within ourselves. Children can ask: "Was I lazy about my school work or tasks at home; did I cheat at school; did I go to bed on time; am I greedy; have I been envious when something good happened to someone else?"

The third area to think about is our behaviour towards other people. So children might ask themselves: "Do I remember to say thank you; did I do what my parents or teachers asked me to do; did I hurt anyone by what I said or did; did I get angry or start a fight; did I get other people into trouble; do I forgive others when they say sorry or do I hold a grudge; do I share my things?"

When we examine our conscience, we also need to consider whether our sins are small (venial) or serious (mortal). Mortal sins destroy the life of God within us. In order for a sin to be mortal it has to meet three criteria. It needs to be: (1) serious; (2) committed intentionally; (3) done with full knowledge of its seriousness. Missing Mass on Sunday is serious and is a mortal sin if you could easily have gone to Mass but deliberately chose not to even though you knew it was seriously wrong. If we intentionally miss Mass on Sunday, we can go to Mass the following week, but we must go to confession before we receive Holy Communion again.

In confession we must confess any mortal sin we might have committed. It is also helpful to confess any smaller sins that we can remember. We are not going to remember every single one, which is why it is usual to say after listing our sins: "For these sins and for all those I do not now remember, I am sorry." We should understand that whatever we have done wrong, God will always forgive and forget, as long as we are truly sorry.

Although making an examination of conscience is associated with preparing for confession, it is not limited to this. A regular, daily habit of examination of conscience helps us to prepare in advance for confession, and also helps us to put things right and make amends as soon as possible after they have gone wrong.

Can a priest tell anyone else your sins?

No! Only, you, God and the priest will ever know your sins. Priests are bound by what we call the 'seal of confession'. If a priest was to reveal the sins of a particular person that he had heard in confession (even if it was the worst sin imaginable) he would not be allowed to be a priest anymore.

How often do I need to go to confession?

If possible, we should go to confession on a regular basis; for example, once a month. However, it is good to say sorry to God as soon as we realise that we have done something wrong, especially if it is a mortal sin. Even if it is quite a small sin it is good to say: "Jesus, I'm sorry", straightaway; then, when we can, to go to confession.

The best way to encourage our children to go to confession is by going ourselves. A good practice is to go together as a family and then perhaps have a family treat afterwards. If children get into the habit of going to confession regularly when they are young and are helped to see it as something very positive then, when they grow up, they are more likely to keep up the good habit.

Points to ponder

• Do we set a good example of forgiveness to our children? Do we ask for forgiveness and forgive others readily?

• How do we prepare for confession? How do we help our children prepare for confession?

Practical application

• Try to establish the good habit of going to confession regularly; perhaps plan in advance a time to go.

• Try to get into the habit of suggesting that your children examine their conscience regularly; that way it does not seem so difficult to prepare for confession.

• Try to make sure that your children are confident with what they should say in confession. They can always take a book or paper with the words on to help them.

• Smile when you have been to confession and encourage your children to do the same! You never know when this positive reaction might well be the encouragement that helps others make the decision to go.

• Mark the day you go to confession with a special treat.

by Daisy Line, Year 4

9. The Bible

Who wrote the Bible?

The Bible is a collection of books written down by many people, but inspired by God. There are seventy-three books in the Catholic Bible. The Old Testament, the first part of the Bible, dates back more than a thousand years before Christ. In addition to the stories of Adam and Eve, Cain and Abel, and Noah, we hear about how God chose Abraham to be the father of a great nation, Israel. We also learn that the Israelites became slaves in Egypt and that God called Moses to lead them out of Egypt to the Promised Land. Also, we hear how over the centuries the Israelites strayed from God, despite all the prophets and other great leaders he sent to them, until finally they were conquered by foreign nations and taken into exile. It was another seventy years before they were able to return to Israel and another four hundred years before God sent his son, Jesus. The Old Testament prepares for the coming of Jesus, and finds its completion and fulfilment in him.

The second part of the Bible, called the New Testament, records the life of Jesus (in the Gospels) and the early Church (the Acts). It contains many letters written by the earliest Christians, especially St Paul. The end of the New Testament tells of how Jesus will return and God will bring to completion what he began in Creation.

The Old and New Testament were written in Hebrew and Greek. In the 4th century, St Jerome was asked by the Pope of the time, Damasus I, to translate the Bible into Latin. None of the original books of the Bible remain today because they were written on papyrus (an early form of paper made from grass) which does not survive well. There are, however, fragments of the Bible texts still existing from as early as AD 120. Through careful investigation, experts know that the versions we have today are very close to the original and fully reliable.

Why do we read the Bible?

We read the Bible because it is the Christian guide book to life and it teaches us about God and who we are. When we read and pray with the Bible, we believe that God speaks through it, helping us to understand how he wants us to live. The Bible is incredibly rich in stories that can be understood at different levels. Even very young children can learn about the creator-God who loves and cares for his people.

The key stories in the Bible are about love, trust, promises broken and kept, doing wrong and being forgiven. They are stories about people who even though they lived a very long time ago, can still teach us important lessons today.

Do we have to take the Bible literally?

Some stories in the Bible are not meant to be taken literally, whereas others are. The stories in the New Testament that tell us we are like branches and Jesus the vine and that we are the salt of the earth, are not meant to be taken literally. Here, God is using familiar images to help us understand how we should live our lives. When we think of salt we think of flavouring food; so here Jesus is asking us to have the quality of salt and to be someone who helps to draw out the good in others. When we think of a vine with branches, we can visualise how branches are connected to the main plant or vine. Here, Jesus is asking us to stay 'connected' to him.

By contrast, other stories should be taken literally. So when Jesus said at the Last Supper, "This is my body, take it and eat it," he does not mean that the bread represents his body; he means that it has truly become his body. It is helpful to understand what kind of literature a particular book of the Bible represents. Sometimes the style is a mix of symbolism and history, as in the book of Genesis. It is also important to understand that the Bible has levels of spiritual meaning which go beyond the literal sense of the words.

Why are there four Gospels?

Having four Gospels is a bit like having four different portraits of Jesus painted by different artists; they help us to see Jesus from slightly different points of view. The Gospels tell us mainly about the last three years of Jesus' life, when he did his most important work as a teacher and healer. Each Gospel tells us something different about Jesus. Although Matthew, Mark and Luke are similar, John is quite different; he tells us, for instance, more about the Last Supper than the other Gospel writers.

Like the Old Testament, the contents of the Gospels were initially passed on verbally. They were written down fully in their present form between thirty to seventy years after Jesus' death. When they were written down, the authors were not trying to write comprehensive biographies of Jesus, nor were they writing history books. Instead, the authors wrote them to share the faith and to testify to the truth about Jesus. Differences in the detail and emphasis between stories arise not only because the authors were different, but because they were writing for very different communities.

Why does Jesus teach in parables?

Jesus spoke in parables because they were clever, memorable stories about everyday life of the time that made people think and usually had a twist at the end to drive the point home. Jesus talked to the ordinary people of the time about things they understood; like sheep, wheat, money and wine. When we think about stories we find most memorable, they usually begin with something that hooks our attention and often have a twist at the end. When someone is teaching us a new subject, it is often easier to understand if they use images that we are familiar with to help explain the newer, more unfamiliar topic. Jesus employed similar storytelling and teaching techniques two thousand years ago!

How do miracles happen?

Miracles happen when God intervenes in the physical world. The laws of nature are not broken by a miracle, but instead, what we would expect to happen is suspended. For example, if someone is diagnosed with a serious, incurable illness but then recovers completely and immediately after prayer without medical treatment, death from the disease has been, in human terms, prevented inexplicably. Jesus performed miracles to show that he was God. Only God could walk on water, multiply loaves and fish, expel demons, give sight to the blind, hearing to the deaf and raise the dead! That these events do not happen often is what makes them miracles.

Points to ponder

- What is your favourite passage from the Bible? Why is it important to you?

- How often do we read the Bible? If not often, could we make more time to do so?

- Do we read the Bible as a family? If not, might we be able to incorporate this into our weekly plan of family activities?

Practical application

• Tell your children about your favourite Bible story; explain why it is important to you or why you particularly like it.

• Consider reading the Bible with your children, perhaps now and again as a bedtime story. Keep a children's Bible to hand, perhaps on the bookshelf with their other story books.

• Teach your children to pray with the Bible (see section on Prayer).

• Over time, collect a list of the parables or miracles you come across when you read the Bible together with your children.

• Read the same story from different Gospels and play a 'spot the difference' game. How many similarities and differences can you find?

• Include Bible story DVDs in your DVD collection. Find an opportunity to watch them, maybe as part of a family Lenten or Advent promise to find out more about God's people and their history.

10. Catholic Devotions

Why do we have holy pictures and statues?

Often we have holy pictures and statues because we have a special devotion to a certain representation of Jesus (maybe as the Sacred Heart) or to Mary (perhaps as Our Lady of Perpetual Help), or to a particular saint (maybe the saint after whom we are named).

Devotions are prayers and customs that can help us extend our prayer life beyond the time we spend at Mass on Sunday. Whilst the Mass is the centre of our friendship with God, other prayers and customs can help us to get to know and love God even better. Good examples of such devotions include: praying the Rosary, the Angelus, the guardian angel prayer, or a novena; saying grace before meals, wearing a Miraculous Medal, making the Stations of the Cross, and going on a pilgrimage or venerating relics. Some of these devotions and customs have been mentioned in other sections and a few more will be mentioned here.

Devotions act a bit like 'spiritual vitamins' to supplement our primary form of nourishment and communication with God, which is the Mass. Like vitamins, devotions are optional; we can take them or leave them although having some can be helpful. Over the centuries a wide range of customs and traditions have developed that, when used well, can help to strengthen our friendship with God and help us to pray more frequently.

Devotions do not take us away from God. On the contrary, God is pleased when we honour his mother and friends who are saints in heaven. Whilst we do not need to ask these holy people to intercede for us, if God has given us so many special friends it seems only sensible to ask them for help when we need it. This is the plan of God. All good devotions and customs should lead us to Jesus. Devotions must also conform to the laws and norms of the Church. Some unapproved devotions can border on superstition, such as hanging Rosary beads on the washing line to ward off rain on your wedding day! This approach to devotions overlooks the point of a prayer as beautiful and profound as the Rosary. Chain prayers that expect us to ask a certain number of people to say a particular prayer, often within a certain time frame, are also superstitious. Bargaining with God is not true devotion.

by Finton Lyons, Year 6

Why do we wear holy medals?

A blessed medal with a holy image on one or both sides is usually worn to honour the person shown on the medal. A blessed medal which is also known as a 'sacramental' (as are many other blessed religious objects and actions) will also bring God's blessing to the wearer. One well-known medal is the Miraculous Medal (see the section on Mary).

Why do we say grace?

Saying grace, a special prayer before meal times, reminds us that God is present in all aspects of our daily lives including eating! Saying grace also creates a sense of thankfulness. Indeed, the term "grace" comes from the Latin word meaning 'thanks'.

What is the Angelus?

The Angelus is a prayer that is traditionally said three times a day at 6am, noon and 6pm. Often a church bell would ring to remind people to pray. "Angelus" is the Latin word for 'angel' and the prayer reminds us of the Incarnation when the Archangel Gabriel appeared to Mary to tell her that she would be the mother of Jesus. The prayer consists of three verses and responses; after each, a Hail Mary is recited and finally, a short concluding prayer said. The Angelus might seem like a very traditional prayer, but it is timeless. The Incarnation is as central to our faith today as it was in the past and will be in the future; and reciting the Angelus, daily, is a wonderful way to proclaim this truth.

What is a novena?

A novena is a particular prayer, or set of prayers, said for nine consecutive days often for a special intention. The word 'novena' is derived from the Latin word meaning 'nine'. The nine days represent the length of time that Mary and the disciples spent in prayer in the Upper Room from the time when Our Lord ascended into heaven until the eve of Pentecost when the Holy Spirit descended upon them. There are many different novenas: to Our Lady, the Holy Spirit and to the saints. Novenas can also be said in preparation for feasts such as Christmas, Easter or the feast day of a saint. Other novenas can be said at any time of the year and might well be said for an urgent need or special request. Whether or not the problem prayed for resolves, the time spent in prayer fills our life with grace and brings us closer to God.

What is a relic?

A relic is usually a tiny part of a saint's body (such as a bone fragment, blood, hair or nail), or often a small piece of clothing. Relics are not gory; they are simply physical reminders of the saints in heaven. Many early Christian communities were centred on the tombs of martyrs. However, as the numbers of Christians increased and were to be found in more places, the remains of martyrs and saints were often broken up and distributed to these new communities so that they too could be physically connected to the great saints of the past. Our Catholic faith is very physical, and objects we can touch or see play an important part in it. Relics also prompt us to ask the saint to intercede before God on our behalf. Relics do not have magical powers, so when a miracle happens it is always the power of God working through the saint.

What is a pilgrimage?

A pilgrimage is a journey to a holy place that we can make for many reasons but often because we have a special devotion to the person or saint associated with the place. We might also go because we wish to ask the saint to intercede for us or in thanksgiving for a blessing we have received. The Christian tradition of pilgrimages began shortly after Jesus' death and resurrection because the early Christians deeply desired to visit the places where Jesus had lived and died. From earliest times, Rome was also a pilgrimage destination and many pilgrims braved the dangers of the pagan city to pray at the tombs of St Peter and St Paul. Later, many more shrines developed, often around the relics of saints. Nowadays, pilgrimages to places associated with apparitions of Our Lady are also extremely popular.

Points to ponder

• What devotions do we observe in our family?

• Are there devotions that we remember from our own childhood that we could introduce to our family today?

• Could we, as a family, research Catholic devotions and customs and choose a new family devotion?

Practical application

• Encourage your children to say grace at meal times. Either use a well-known version or perhaps come up with your own family version.

• Teach your children the Angelus and perhaps say it when possible as a family.

• Consider making a pilgrimage as a family. It does not have to be to a faraway destination, maybe there is a church nearby associated with a saint or martyr that you could visit? Find out about the saint before you go.

• Perhaps also select a few devotions suggested in other sections, such as praying the Rosary and saying the guardian angel prayer, to add to your family collection of devotions.

CATHOLIC LIFE
AND TIMES

by Isobel Lane, Year 5

11. Advent and Christmas

What does Advent mean?

'Advent' meaning 'coming' in Latin and describes the weeks of preparation before Christmas. Advent always includes four Sundays and so it is three weeks long if Christmas falls on a Monday, or four weeks if on a Saturday. The reason we use a word that means 'coming' to describe this time is because it is about preparing for the coming of Christ. Naturally, our main focus tends to be on our preparations for Christmas, which is the anniversary of Christ coming to us over two thousand years ago through his birth in Bethlehem. However, Advent is also a time when we prepare to receive Christ better in the many ways that he comes to us, here and now. That is, in the Eucharist, through the Word of God, through grace and in the poor and suffering. Finally, Advent is also a time when we think about whether we are properly prepared to meet God when we die and for the coming of Christ in the future, at the end of time.

Advent is the beginning of the Church's year and we move into a new cycle of prayer, liturgy and scripture. Advent is a good time to reflect on the new beginnings that we can make in our lives. In fact, Advent is actually a bit like a mini-Lent. During Advent it is good to mark our new beginning in three ways: by giving up something we like, helping others more and making extra time for prayer.

The time before Christmas can be a difficult one to give up a favourite food or drink, but one that is really worthwhile if we can manage. Fasting is one of the most powerful and time-honoured forms of Christian prayer. Jesus said that fasting accomplishes what other prayers cannot. Some of the best ways to help others at any time, but especially during Advent, can be to offer a helping hand, an encouraging word or even just to make an extra effort to smile more. Also, giving a donation to a special charity is a good way to help others in Advent and reminds us that Christmas is about giving to others. If we have plenty, we have a special responsibility to give to others.

One of the most powerful prayers during Advent is to attend weekday Mass. After all, Advent is a time when we prepare for 'Christ-Mass', literally the Mass of Christ. Also, the Eucharist strengthens us at a time when we might well experience extra pressures at home, school or work, tricky family dynamics and possibly too many social engagements. Apart from going to Mass, Advent is a time when we can try to increase our personal and family prayer, and also try to go to confession.

Why does the priest wear purple in Advent?

Purple is the colour of penance and the purple vestments worn in Advent help to remind us of the extra effort that we try to make to be properly prepared for the coming of Christ. Advent started in the 6th century as a time for physical, spiritual and mental preparation for Christmas, but it was celebrated differently in different countries. In France it was a rather solemn time of fasting, whereas in Rome the Sundays leading up to Christmas were a time of joyful celebration. Now, we have a mixture of both: penance mixed with joy, signified by the joyful celebration on the third Sunday of Advent, called Gaudete Sunday. On this day the priest can wear brighter, rose-coloured vestments instead of purple ones to mark the occasion.

Why do we have Advent wreaths?

Strange though it may seem, the tradition of Advent wreaths came from the practice of replacing the wheels of wagons with snow runners when summer changed to winter in Northern Europe! The wheels were stored on the walls inside the houses to protect them from the harsh weather. They were also decorated with evergreen and candles. This is how the tradition of the Advent wreath began. Each component of the wreath is symbolic. The circle represents eternity and God's unending love. The evergreen symbolises everlasting life and the candles represent Jesus the light of the world.

Who invented the Christmas crib?

St Francis of Assisi, whose love of animals is well known, introduced the practice of depicting the Nativity scene as a three-dimensional setting in the 13th century. One year, just before Christmas, in the woods outside Greccio near Assisi, St Francis decided to re-enact the Nativity scene with real animals. He particularly desired to be able to visualise the infant Jesus lying in the manger between an ox and a donkey. People came from all around to visit the scene and to rejoice in and celebrate the birth of Christ. From this time on, the custom of the Christmas crib spread all over the Christian world.

Who is Saint Nicholas?

St Nicholas was a bishop who lived in Turkey in the 4th century. He is the patron saint of children and his feast is celebrated on 6th December. He was a role model of generosity and loved giving money to the poor. It is said that he threw money through a window of one particular house to provide a dowry (wedding money) for three girls. In many countries there is a tradition that St Nicholas brings gifts to children on the eve of his feast day. St Nicholas also had a special devotion to the infant Jesus and once even risked his life to save an image of the Holy Infant from a burning church.

Why do we give gifts at Christmas?

At Christmas we give gifts to our family and friends to celebrate Jesus' birthday. Jesus does not need material gifts, but as a sign of our love for him we give gifts to others and this makes him very happy. It can be helpful to make a 'give list' to remind us that Christmas is about giving to others, not just about receiving. If you also make a 'wish list', a good place to put it is by the crib for the angels to take to heaven!

Why do we have Christmas trees?

Decorated Christmas trees bring light and beauty into our homes and we use them to honour Christ's birth. A mixture of history and legend tell us that St Boniface, an English saint from Devon who went as a missionary to Germany in the 8th century, was the first to suggest that a fir tree be decorated to mark the birth of Christ. St Boniface wanted to prevent trees being worshipped and seen as magical beings, and so cut down the tree of the pagan god Woden. However, as he also understood the need to preserve what was good in the old pre-Christian customs, he devised a way to incorporate the tree into a Christian tradition. A fir tree is an evergreen and thus symbolises immortality. When a Christmas tree is lit up, we are reminded of the light Jesus brought into the world when he was born.

What are the Twelve days of Christmas?

The twelve days of Christmas are the days from Christmas Day until 5th January, the eve of the Epiphany and the feast that commemorates the arrival of the three kings in Bethlehem. The song, 'The Twelve Days of Christmas' reminds us that the whole Christmas season is meant to be a time of celebration. It is sad when the Christmas tree and crib are taken down a few days after 25th December and Christmas all but forgotten. Traditionally, the Christmas season extends as far as the feast of Candlemas (2nd February) when Our Lord was presented in the temple by Our Lady and St Joseph.

Points to ponder

• Do we take time to reflect on the meaning of Advent and Christmas ourselves, so to be better able to explain them to our children?

• How do we show our children that the Advent season should be about love of Christ, prayer, personal holiness and some penance? Can we use customs and traditions to strengthen this attitude?

Practical application

• There are lots of helpful Advent customs in addition to the one we are most familiar with: the Advent calendar. Perhaps select one or two Advent traditions that you think might help your family prepare for Christmas. A few examples are as follows:

  ○ You might decide to buy or perhaps make an Advent wreath. Three of the candles on an Advent wreath are generally purple, with a fourth being pink for the third Sunday of Advent, Gaudete Sunday. A fifth (white) candle is placed in the centre and is lit on Christmas Day. The more candles we light on the wreath, the more light we bring into our home, the more we are reminded to rejoice because the birth of Christ is near. There are lots of different ways an Advent wreath can be used. One way is to light it at meal times and perhaps pray for a different person or situation every day.

○ You could make and decorate a Jesse Tree, which is a symbolic or pictorial representation of Jesus' family tree. There are lots of ways to do this but a very simple one is to start by drawing a picture of a large, branching tree. On each day of Advent read (usually in chronological order) one of the Bible stories (or just a verse or two) which tells of the people and events of Jesus' ancestors. At the same time draw and colour on your tree a picture to represent the story. By tracing Jesus' earthly ancestor back to Jesse, the father of King David, and beyond, we are helped to see Jesus as a real, historical figure.

○ With younger children you might enjoy the custom of preparing a manger; that is, making a soft, comfortable bed for baby Jesus. Every time a family member does a good deed (for example, says a kind word or prayer for another person) a piece of straw or cotton wool can be placed in a manger (for example, an empty shoe box). When the Christ Child comes on Christmas Eve he will find plenty of bedding to keep him warm and soften the hardness of his manger.

○ In addition to a more ornamental crib, non-breakable/child friendly crib figures are a great way for children to become familiar with the Christmas story. They can set them up and move them around as often as they like.

• As a family decide together what to give up for Advent and encourage one another to keep commitments made.

• Deciding, as a family, to give an extra donation to a special charity is also a helpful way of preparing for Christmas.

• Watch a Christmas story DVD and/or read a Christmas story book with your children.

by Serena Johannes, Year 5

12. Lent and Easter

Why do we have Lent?

We observe Lent because it gives us a special time each year to make changes for the better and improve our friendship with God and others. Lent lasts for six weeks (forty ordinary days and six Sundays) before Easter Sunday. The length of time represents the forty days Jesus spent in the desert, fasting and praying before starting his public life and ministry.

The three key areas that we concentrate on during Lent are prayer, fasting and almsgiving. We might decide to pray more by going to Mass once or twice during the week or by saying the Rosary more frequently. We fast by giving up something we like (sweets, biscuits) or a bad habit (complaining, grumbling). Strange though it may seem, fasting is also a very powerful form of prayer. Finally, we give alms either by collecting money for charity or by giving others our time or talents, perhaps by helping more at home or visiting a sick friend or relative. Almsgiving is important not only because we help others, but also because it is a very effective way of making up for our sins. When we do something wrong, not only should we say sorry; we need to make up for what we have done.

Why do we give up things for Lent?

One reason we give up things that we like or bad habits is because the sacrifice involved joins our suffering (often associated with doing something we find hard) with Jesus' suffering, and this strengthens our friendship with God. Another reason is that being strong and persevering with our Lenten resolutions helps to makes us stronger in other areas of our life; the combined effect is to change us for the better.

Why do we eat pancakes on Shrove Tuesday?

Pancakes are made with eggs, which years ago were considered a luxury item; as Lent is a time of fasting, luxuries (such as eggs) were used up on Shrove Tuesday, the day before Lent begins. In some countries Shrove Tuesday is called 'Mardi Gras' or 'Fat Tuesday.' Again, this comes from the tradition of eating up all the good food on the day before Lent begins. Other customs associated with Shrove Tuesday in some countries are carnivals and parades. Carnival comes from two Latin words: 'carne' meaning 'meat' and 'vale' meaning 'goodbye,' and refers to the old tradition of giving up meat in Lent. Masks are often worn at the carnivals to symbolise the barrier we create between ourselves and God. Removing the mask on the stroke of midnight, just before Lent starts, symbolises a new start and our resolution to improve our friendship with God.

Why do we have ashes put on our forehead on Ash Wednesday?

On Ash Wednesday the priest makes a sign of the cross on our forehead with ashes to remind us that it is the beginning of Lent because blessed ashes are a symbol of sorrow and mourning. The ashes are made by burning the palms left over from Palm Sunday the previous year.

Ash Wednesday is a day that the Church tells us that all Catholics from the end of their fourteenth year should abstain from eating meat and meat products. Generally, everyone over the age of eighteen, until the end of their fifty-ninth year, whom are well and healthy, must also fast (only eat one main meal and two light snacks) on Ash Wednesday.

Why is it good to go to confession in Lent?

It is good to go to confession in Lent particularly, if we can, near the beginning because if we are going to try to change for the better, then saying sorry to God for our sins in confession is the best possible start. The word 'Shrove' in Shrove Tuesday comes from the word 'shrive' meaning to be rid of our sins. It was customary to ring the shriving bell on the Tuesday before Lent to call everyone to confession. Another good reason we go to confession during Lent is that we are asked by the Church to attend confession at least once a year. The recommended time for this is from the beginning of Lent up until the end of the Easter season, at Pentecost; not to go at least once a year can itself be a mortal sin.

When is Palm Sunday?

Palm Sunday is the Sunday before Easter Sunday and is the beginning of Holy Week. It is the day that we remember Jesus' triumphant entry into Jerusalem when the crowds broke branches from the trees to wave and also to make a carpet for Jesus' donkey to ride on. Tradition tells us that every donkey has a cross marked on its back because a donkey carried Jesus on the first Palm Sunday. When Palm Sunday was celebrated in the 4th century, the worshippers used to hold up olive twigs during the procession. It was not until several hundred years later that palm branches were used. Nowadays, on this day there is a procession at Mass, palms are blessed and held in the air, and people sing or say "Hosanna" just as they did in Jerusalem two thousand years ago.

Why are the statues covered during Holy Week?

During Holy Week the statues and crucifixes in the church are covered with purple cloth to remind us that we are in mourning. Also, the statues and pictures are a sign of beauty, and when they are covered it helps us to focus on the passion and death of Jesus.

Why do we go to church three times at Easter?

The liturgies of Holy Thursday, Good Friday and the Easter Vigil form one extended Liturgy so we go three times to hear all the parts that make up the whole. This is why we are encouraged to go to all three. 'Triduum' is a Latin word that means 'three days' and is the official name given to these days.

Why does the priest wash people's feet on Holy Thursday?

The priest washes the feet of some parishioners to repeat Jesus' action at the Last Supper when he washed the feet of the apostles. Another name for Holy Thursday is Maundy Thursday. 'Maundy' comes from the Latin word 'mandatum', which means command. The command that Jesus gave us at the Last Supper was that we must love one another. To show us what he meant by service to others being at the heart of love, Jesus washed the feet of his apostles before supper began. The washing of the feet on Holy Thursday is an action that is performed in Catholic churches across the world. Holy Thursday commemorates Jesus' sharing of the Last Supper with his disciples the night before he died and the institution of the Holy Eucharist. It is also the day on which he instituted the holy priesthood.

Why is the tabernacle left open and empty?

After the Mass of the Last Supper, the Blessed Sacrament is not replaced in the tabernacle on the main altar; and the tabernacle door is left open to indicate this. Instead the Blessed Sacrament is moved to a side altar (called the altar of repose) and kept there. Often there is an opportunity to spend some time in front of the altar of repose in adoration before the Blessed Sacrament. This is an opportunity for us to spend time watching and waiting with Jesus. This is what Jesus asked his disciples to do in the garden of Gethsemane, but they fell asleep!

Why is it called Good Friday?

The Friday of Holy Week is called 'Good Friday', but it is likely that it was first called 'God's Friday'. This is the day that we remember God's suffering and death on the cross, and it has been remembered this way since the 4th century. It is also 'Good' in its effects which bring about the salvation of the world. Usually, close to three o'clock, the Lord's Passion is celebrated. The altar is bare and the celebrant enters and makes the dramatic gesture of lying on the floor before the altar and the congregation prays in silence. This act represents the magnitude of what Christ did for us on the cross. After that we listen to the Passion read from St John's Gospel. Next, there is the solemn veneration of the cross and the distribution of Holy Communion, but no Mass is celebrated.

Why do we kiss the cross?

We each kiss the crucifix during the Good Friday Liturgy as a way of thanking Jesus for dying for us to bring us eternal life. Each person comes forward and kisses or touches the cross. When only one cross is used, it underlines the full significance of the symbolism of the rite. The history of the veneration of the cross goes back to early Christianity. In the fourth century, St Helena, mother of the Emperor Constantine, is said to have unearthed three crosses at Golgotha and to have verified through a series of miracles which was the true cross. The incorporation of fragments of the true cross into many early crosses gave rise to the practice of veneration of the cross. This became such a strong devotion throughout Christian history that it is now part of the Good Friday Liturgy.

What are the Stations of the Cross?

The Stations of the Cross are fourteen beautiful meditations about Jesus' journey on the road to Jerusalem towards Calvary which took place on Good Friday. St Francis of Assisi is said to have brought the devotion from the Holy Land. Today, Catholic churches have fourteen Stations (either pictures or sculptures) around the wall of the church. The custom of praying the Stations is particularly associated with Fridays in Lent. It is a powerful way to remember what Jesus did for us and to help us get closer to him.

Why is there no Mass on Holy Saturday?

There is no Mass on Holy Saturday because it is the day we remember and reflect on the time Jesus spent in the tomb. Holy Saturday lasts until dusk after which the Easter Vigil is celebrated, marking the official start of the Easter season.

Why is there a bonfire at the Easter Vigil?

The Easter Vigil begins with the lighting of a fire because it symbolises the change that happens to us during Lent. Fire changes the form of objects, for example solid metal can melt in the heat of a fire. A Paschal (Easter) candle is lit from the fire to represent the Risen Christ and is carried into a darkened church. The dark is dispelled gradually as we all light our candles from the Paschal candle. As we hold our lighted candles at the beginning of the Easter season we can take a few moments to think about how we might have grown closer to God through our Lenten preparations.

Why do we give Easter eggs as presents?

We give eggs as presents at Easter because an egg symbolises new life, in this case the eternal life Christ gave us by dying and rising again. The hard and seemingly lifeless-looking shell of an egg represents the stone tomb from which the risen Christ emerged, bringing us eternal life. The Easter egg is one of the most widely recognised Easter symbols but, because it has been widely secularised, it is easy to forget that Easter eggs symbolise the Resurrection. Another reason eggs are associated with Easter is that real eggs used to be considered a luxury and were forbidden in Lent, so it became customary to give eggs as presents at Easter. The first eggs given were bird's eggs that were painted and decorated. It is still a popular activity for children today to decorate hard-boiled eggs for Easter. When the first chocolate eggs were produced they were the size of a small bird's egg. Now, many are as large as ostrich eggs!

Points to ponder

• How do we prepare ourselves and our family during Lent? Do we have well-established family traditions or could we use one or two of the ideas suggested here to help us?

• How do we celebrate Easter as a family? How do we mark its importance?

Practical application

• Choose one or two ways to prepare during Lent as a family. Here are a few suggestions:

  ○ Make a Lenten map to help you remember the good deeds and little sacrifices that you hope to do and make during Lent. Take a large piece of card and forty-six squares of coloured paper (to represent forty ordinary days and six Sundays) and stick them on the card in the shape of a winding path. On each day, write a task (for example, say an extra prayer for someone, do a good deed, do not eat sweets). When you have completed the task cover the square with a sticker: a smiley face or a heart perhaps. Sometimes we get lost on a journey. A map helps us get to our destination. Lent is like a long journey and it can be quite easy to get lost and forget our resolutions. A map can be very helpful for our Lenten journey.

○ Create a Lenten tree decorated with colourful paper butterflies, where each butterfly represents a Lenten sacrifice or good deed done. There are several reasons for using butterflies. First, a butterfly starts life as a caterpillar and this process symbolises the change which can happen to each of us during Lent. Second, a butterfly emerges from a chrysalis and this symbolises Christ emerging from the tomb. To start the Lenten tree, put a few small branches or large twigs in a vase. Make caterpillars by cutting up pipe cleaners (fat furry ones work well) and tie a piece of string or strong thread to each. Hang the caterpillars on the branches. Cut out butterflies from coloured paper and attach thread. When a family member carries out a Lenten promise, replace a caterpillar with a butterfly. By Easter the tree will be covered in beautiful butterflies. This project could be used alone or in conjunction with a Lenten map.

○ Use an alms box to collect money during Lent to donate to a good cause. Children are often given alms boxes to bring home from school. Otherwise you can make a simple one by decorating a jam jar, tin or small box. When family members make a small sacrifice such as not buying sweets or foregoing a trip to the cinema, the money saved can be put into the alms box.

• Try if possible to go as a family to the Stations of the Cross during Lent. Explain to your children that we say the Stations as a reminder that Jesus gave his life to save us. Perhaps at another time when the church is empty, walk around the Stations together pointing out the events represented. Several of the Stations show Jesus falling down because the cross was so heavy; others show people who tried to help Jesus on his journey. The twelfth Station shows Jesus hanging on the cross; the last one shows Jesus being placed in the tomb.

by Dominic Kohashikawa, Year 6

13. Children's Literature

Why do I have to read?

There are lots of reasons to read, but one is that reading and listening to stories provides the best possible training for our imagination. Our imagination is a part of our soul and a gift God gives us to help us make sense of the world. When we visualise pictures of people, things or events in our minds, it helps to form our imagination. Images imprint in our mind the way that an object held tight in the hand can leave a mark on the palm. Images formed in the imagination are very effective because they can stay in our memory a long time after we have forgotten words and explanations.

Books are a very powerful way of transferring human experience from the mind of an author to the reader. Whilst authors have a very responsible and influential position in forming children's imagination, the role parents play is fundamental because we can guide our children's reading. Empowering children's imaginations with good quality books is one way to counterbalance some of the more negative influences of popular culture.

Why are there baddies in some stories?

The bad guys in stories are generally defeated in the end and including baddies in stories helps us to remember this important fact. Children are fascinated by stories that maintain moral order in which good defeats evil. Children gain security from knowing that there are standards that they and others are expected to live up to. They understand that the bad guys in stories are the ones who do not live up to these standards. Good literature that depicts this moral order can help to clarify good and evil for children.

Why is it so important that children are exposed to clear examples or moral order through books and literature? In today's society moral principles are losing their objective standards, that is, standards that are universal, the same for everyone. Instead, now what often happens is that something that is wrong when one person does it, might not be considered wrong when another does. To take a simple example, it is wrong for you to deliberately stamp hard on someone's foot and hurt them. But imagine if it was acceptable for another person to do this perhaps because it was part of their culture. How would you know when it was right or wrong? Standards are becoming relative and dependent on social, cultural and personal circumstances. This intellectual current is known as moral relativism and is considered by some as the most destructive force of our times.

Children exposed to good books in which moral order is maintained and is the same for everyone are helped to develop the habit of seeing and understanding the difference between good and evil. Good and evil have not changed in today's world.

Why are fairies usually good?

In fantasy stories fairies usually represent good characters and witches bad ones because this provides us with a consistent and familiar framework, and maintains the order we expect. In the real world we understand events and situations of life through the images that form in our mind from concrete experiences. For example, a dog with a terrifying snarl and large sharp teeth inevitably suggests danger which we learn to avoid. But this is not so easy with the invisible world of God, angels and evil spirits because we cannot see them. Instead, we need symbols we can see to represent the features of the invisible world. This then helps us to form the images in our mind that we need to help us react appropriately. A fire-breathing dragon or a poisonous-looking snake representing Satan is an appropriate symbol because the images imprinted in our mind suggest danger and evil. Symbolism in traditional fantasy stories generally uses witches to represent evil characters and fairies, good ones. When symbolism is blurred, reversed and loses its traditional meaning, we can begin to forget that evil exists.

Why are magical stories sometimes scary?

If stories about magic are scary it is often because they are occult stories that include paranormal events. Fantasy and occult stories both use magic and sometimes it can be difficult to tell them apart. In general, in a traditional fantasy story the action takes place in an unreal world, but the depth of the story is real. Children walk through wardrobes or fall through pictures into other worlds but these are worlds in which moral order exists. Also, the heroes fight using fair and not foul means, and good triumphs in the end. Good examples of these types of stories include the many books by Christian authors J.R.R. Tolkien and C.S. Lewis. By contrast, in occult stories terrifying occurrences and phenomena take place in the real world. When moral order is missing and the power of evil outweighs that of good children can be scared and disturbed.

Points to ponder

• What books do our children read? If we do not know the book or author do we take a few moments to find out about them?

• How do we guide our children in what they read? Can we strike a balance between what they enjoy reading and what we think might be helpful for them to read?

Practical application

• Ask your children how they visualise things they cannot see. Perhaps use images in the church and from the Mass as examples. Incense is a way to visualise prayers going up to heaven and the lit sanctuary lamp reminds us that Jesus is in the tabernacle.

• Talk to your children about how their imagination is formed. Illustrate the point with the example of holding an object tightly in your hand for a few moments and then looking to see if it leaves a temporary mark or imprint in the palm.

• If possible read with your children and discuss the story, characters and meaning.

• Take time to tell stories to your children, either make believe or true stories from your own childhood.

14. Cultivating Virtue

Why do I have to be good?

More often than not, when we are not good we end up hurting someone; either ourselves, others or God. Trying to be good and learning good habits can reduce the times that we hurt ourselves and others. Good habits come from the inclination within us to carry out good actions and are called 'virtues'. We can develop virtues through repeated good actions. However, we also need God's grace through prayer and the sacraments to help us acquire and practise the virtues successfully, and for the right reasons.

All good habits are linked to the four main virtues of prudence, fortitude, temperance and justice. Together, they are known as the cardinal virtues. This word comes from the Latin word *'cardo'* which means 'hinge'. A hinge is that part of the door that helps it open and close, that is, to work properly. The cardinal virtues are the hinges that help our lives work properly and that help us live a good life and behave well towards others.

The virtue of prudence helps us to decide the right thing to do in any given situation. Justice helps us make sure that everyone has what rightfully belongs to them. Fortitude is the virtue that helps us to do the right thing, even when it seems very hard. Finally, the virtue of temperance helps us to be self-disciplined in all that we do.

As well as the four cardinal virtues there are three theological virtues which are gifts we receive from God when we are baptised. The theological virtues are faith, hope and charity (love). Faith helps us to believe what God tells us, no matter how impossible it might seem. A good example of this is our belief that the bread and wine of the Eucharist really become the Body and Blood of Jesus at the consecration. Hope is about trusting in God at all times. Even when things seem really bad, we trust that God has not abandoned us, and that good can come from difficult circumstances. Charity helps us to love God above all things and others because that is what God asks us to do. What is truly great about the gifts of faith, hope and love is that unlike other presents they do not break, get lost or wear out; in fact, the more we use them the better they get!

Many of the questions children ask concerning behaviour relate to virtues. Here are some examples and an explanation of the virtues to which such question relate.

Why do I have to do what you say?

Learning to do as we are told helps us to grow in the virtue of obedience. Very often obedience is seen as our freewill being controlled by someone else and this seems to be the very opposite of freedom. However difficult it might be to understand, obedience is actually the source of true freedom because we are free to choose how to respond. Obeying a command, provided what we are being asked to do is good and just, has several consequences. First, it is a sign of love and affection for our parents or a mark of respect for a figure of authority. Second, obeying a command can keep us safe. If we are told to stay on the pavement and look each way before crossing the road, then this is sound advice. Third, if we learn to obey our parents when we are young, when we are older we are more likely to respond, positively, to God when he calls us to a particular way of life.

When we teach our children obedience it is essential that the experience is situated within the context of values we consider important. If we value punctuality then we would expect our children to be ready when we ask them to be. However, if we try to enforce obedience in every minute detail, for example doing something our way when several ways are equally good, then it becomes difficult for a child to work out what is important and what is not, and the tendency to be disobedient can increase.

Why do I have to say "please" and "thank you"?

We say please and thank you because they are a way of showing respect for others. The virtue of respect is important not only for society, to help us live harmoniously with others but, also for the whole of creation. We are here to look after the rest of creation, not to use and abuse it.

Also, when we say "please" and as long as we mean it sincerely, we recognise that we are not totally self-sufficient. Often we need help and support from others and we certainly need it from God. Likewise, when we say "thank you" it can help us remember that we also need to thank God. After all, our talents are gifts from God and we need to thank him for our successes. One way we can thank God for all that we have is to try hard to do our best in everything we do each day, and offer it to him as a gesture of thanks.

Why do I have to say "sorry"?

We say sorry when we have offended or mistreated someone because it is likely that we have hurt them physically or emotionally. When we say sorry and genuinely mean what we say it suggests that we understand ourselves and our actions, and we learn to be sincere. Sincerity is the virtue of speaking and acting honestly about our feelings to the appropriate person and at the right time. Sincerity helps us to acknowledge that sometimes the things we do are wrong and that we need to apologise. Another benefit of learning to be sincere is that it helps us make a good confession, to tell God that we are sincerely sorry and to ask for forgiveness.

Why do I have to share?

Sharing and being generous are excellent ways to show our love for others. When we choose, freely, to share our belongings or our time either by helping others or listening to them, we show our love for them. It is often easy to give away things we no longer need or want, but we should always try to give more than just what we have left over. We need to remember that our belongings, gifts and talents are given to us to share. We should also try not to complain if there is something we want but do not have. We do not need a lot of unnecessary belongings.

We should also learn to share and give without expecting something in return. We should try to help those who are less likeable and not only those who are easy to help. We should always be on the lookout for ways we can help others. For instance, at home it might be as simple as putting clothes away or setting the table for a meal without waiting to be asked. Happiness comes from forgetting yourself and serving others. If we serve God and others as generously as we can, God will give us many blessings.

Why do I have to do my homework and tidy my room?

Doing homework and tidying up are about hard work and often perseverance, which is sticking with the task until it is done. When we tidy up we help others, we create order so we can find what we are looking for more easily and we usually feel satisfied because we have a nice, tidy room. When we stick with something we find difficult until it is finished, like our homework or perhaps practising a musical instrument, we can also feel satisfied that our school work gets better or, our instrument playing improves. Work, especially when a job is well done, can give us great satisfaction. Strange though it might seem work is a blessing! Hard work, perseverance and order are really good virtues to learn when we are young because they will help us throughout life.

Why can't I watch what I want on TV?

Not all programmes or films, even ones that are age-appropriate, may reflect our family values. Controlling what our children watch on the television or computer and the magazines they read relates to the virtue of purity. As Catholic parents, we do not need to be killjoys, but we do need to act responsibly about what our children are exposed to through the media, particularly the way love is portrayed. Love is the essence of life and if children watch films that distort love, then not only can it corrupt their understanding of human love but, they risk losing sight of God's love also. St John Bosco, who wrote often on the virtue of purity, stressed the importance of occupying recreation time with worthwhile pursuits and games, which is as relevant for children today as it was when he wrote about it in the 19th century.

Also, connected to the virtue of purity is modesty, particularly in the way our children dress. Modesty in dress is important because we hope that people will look first and foremost at our face because that is where we communicate most.

Why do I have to be patient?

When we lack patience with others we push them away and this is not in the spirit of Jesus. There will always be things that make us impatient, but if we take a moment to think about it there is usually little reason to get cross and angry. There is such a thing as righteous anger, as Jesus showed when he chased the money changers from the temple, but even this must be in proportion to the offence.

Why do I have to know about God?

Learning to grow in affection and love of God is called the virtue of piety. Just as we want to know our parents so we should want to know God who is our true Father, who created us and loves us. As parents our most important task is to help our children grow in love and knowledge of God through encouraging regular prayer, reading the Bible and instilling respect of and devotion to the Eucharist.

Points to ponder

• How do we cultivate virtue in our children? What values do we have as a family? Could we give our children reasonable tasks to help them grow in the virtues that match our family values?

• What virtue do I most lack? How can I improve in this virtue?

Practical application

• Try to remember to model the virtues. Try to set a good example of the behaviour you expect from your children.

• Encourage your children to think daily about what they did well and what they could do better and how. Suggest they also ask God for help to improve in the things that they struggle with.

• Encourage your children to look out for little ways to help others.

15. Vocation and Evangelisation

What is a vocation?

In the general sense, a vocation can be thought of as 'our part in God's plan'. Our vocation is the life God is calling us to lead. Most Catholics associate the word 'vocation' with a calling to the priesthood or religious life and whilst this is an extremely important part of vocation, the word also refers to two other aspects and it is good to understand these as well.

The first aspect is the 'common Christian vocation' and is shared by all members of the Church and comes to us through baptism. We live out our Christian vocation by being committed to the faith, loving and serving God and others, and helping with the saving work of Christ, in other words responding to the universal call to holiness (becoming saints).

The second aspect of vocation refers to our particular 'state in life'; this can be clerical, consecrated (either as a member of a religious order or a lay movement), married or the single lay state. Our state in life is the particular way that each of us will carry out our commitment to a Christian life.

The other aspect of vocation is 'personal vocation', which is the individual and unrepeatable role that God has for each of us to help with the saving work of Christ. Our personal vocation is God's will for us and is built around our strengths, weaknesses, relationships, commitments and obligations. Our personal vocation is expressed through our common Christian vocation and our state in life.

When I grow up, what should I be?

What do you think that God wants you to be when you grow up? We frequently ask our children what they want to be when we should probably be asking them what they think God might want them to be!

Every human being needs to work out what it is that God wishes them to do in life. Parents play a key role in guiding their children to a future hinged on God's will for

by Maddie McHaffie, Year 6

each of them. However, when the time comes it is vital we avoid telling our children what to do or dictating the course we would prefer them to take. Difficult though it might be, God's plan for our children must take precedence over our desires!

How do I know what God wants me to be?

We can work out what God wants us to be, or do, by a process called discernment. Discernment, particularly of our direction in life, can be a complex task that extends over many years. Everyone needs to discern their own personal vocation or path through life. However, beginning the process in our children by helping them to become aware that God has a plan for them which they need to discover and make their own, is an invaluable help. We can point out that the priesthood and consecrated life are possibilities to consider, but implying that the only purpose of discernment is to find out whether God is calling them to be a priest or religious is to misrepresent vocation and limit a child's view of God's plan for them. That said, in learning to search for our personal vocation we are more likely to hear a call to religious life, if that is what God wants. Another point to remember is that God acts first. A personal vocation comes from God together with the grace to make a free commitment to this calling. Whilst God has a plan for our unique co-operation, God never coerces or forces us.

Young children are unlikely to have to make big decisions, but God still expects them to realise that they should learn to be co-operative, kind, respectful and quick to say please and thank you. This helps to foster an environment in which the process of discernment can flourish later on. As children get older they can be encouraged to start asking Jesus what he would wish them to do in aspects of their lives such as making friends, school and other activities. Framing choices in this guise when children are young helps to inform and shape the bigger decisions later. Soon after First Holy Communion and before Confirmation is a really good time for children to start to think about what God might be asking of them.

It is also helpful for children to realise the reason it is important that we find out what God wants for us and why. God has given us everything and Jesus laid down his life for us. By working out our part in God's plan and carrying it out, we can show our gratitude and love to God.

Why do we need to talk about God?

Each and every one of us has a responsibility to pass on the faith. As we pass the faith on to our children, so it becomes their responsibility to pass it on to others. When Jesus died, not very many people knew him. Before he ascended into heaven Jesus asked his disciples to "go out to the whole world; proclaim the Good News to all creation" (Mk 16:15). Gradually, the stories of Jesus were told and retold and the faith began to spread all over the world. We all need to talk about our faith to others to keep the good news of Jesus alive; we call this evangelisation. With all the happiness and love that comes to us from knowing Jesus, how could we possibly keep it to ourselves?

Points to ponder

• What are we here for? How do our children understand their purpose in this world? Is it to be a part of God's saving plan?

• How would we talk to our children about vocation?

Practical application

• Help your child learn about the process of discernment by praying with them to help find out what God wishes for them. Discernment can be helpful with smaller decisions such as deciding whether to keep up a particular hobby or activity and also bigger decisions like the choice of secondary school.

• Try to be a good role model in talking about your faith to others so to encourage your children to do the same.

• In family prayers include a prayer for vocations to the priesthood and consecrated life.

• Keep up customs such as saying grace before meals when friends come to visit. Do not be tempted to move religious objects from sight when visitors call! These can be simple but effective ways of demonstrating our faith.